# With Open Arms

Creating School Communities of Support
for Kids with Social Challenges Using Circle of Friends,
Extracurricular Activities, and Learning Teams

Mary Schlieder, M.S.

Autism Asperger Publishing Co.
P.O. Box 23173
Shawnee Mission, Kansas 66283-0173
www.asperger.net

© 2007 Autism Asperger Publishing Co.
P.O. Box 23173
Shawnee Mission, Kansas 66283-0173
www.asperger.net • 913.897.1004

Publisher's Cataloging-in-Publication

Schlieder, Mary.

    With open arms : creating school communities of support for kids with social challenges using Circle of Friends, extracurricular activities, and learning teams / Mary Schlieder. -- 1st ed. -- Shawnee Mission, Kan. : Autism Asperger Pub. Co., 2007.

        p. ; cm.

        ISBN-13: 978-1-934575-00-0
        ISBN-10: 1-934575-00-3
        LCCN: 2007929035
        Includes bibliographical references.

        1. Children with social disabilities--Education. 2. Autistic children--Education. 3. Autism in children. 4. Teachers of children with social disabilities--Handbooks, manuals, etc. I. Title.

LC4717 .S35 2007                  2007929035
371.94--dc22                  0706

This book is designed in Futura and Souvenir.

Printed in the United States of America.

# With Open Arms

# Dedication

To my sons Ian, Daniel, and Philip,
who continue to motivate and inspire me,
and to my students and mentors –
Caleb, Cassie, Jake, Danny, Dalton,
Darren, and Dylan – who have taught me so much.

# Acknowledgments

Special thanks go to special educator Lisa Brown and paraprofessionals Jan Hart, Lori Hunter, and Donna Erikson, who daily work by my side with optimism and a sense of humor. I would like to express my appreciation to the Norris School District teachers and administrators for giving me the support and freedom to take my ideas and run with them. Thanks to educators Phil Severson, John Votta, Curt Carlson, Kelly Millington, Tom Brazee, Jack Jenkins, and Randy Bates, who never failed to say "yes" when asked to include my students in extracurricular activities, which was often a journey into the unknown. Thanks to Nancy Martin, our library media specialist, who is always able to find just the right book. Thank you also to Matt for being a source of encouragement and hope.

# Table of Contents

# INTRODUCTION

Being 14 years old when my cousin Nate was born, I remember his childhood quite well. A brother of mine was born the same year, so they grew up together, and there was a lot of back-and-forth between our homes.

Nate was a precocious child, with an extensive vocabulary and a fascination with marine biology. While unusual, it was pretty cute the way he could spout off obscure facts in his 4-year-old, high-pitched lisp. He learned to read before kindergarten and spent hours and hours with his science books. But when he started school, his mom became aware of differences she had never encountered with Nate's four older siblings. For one thing, Nate was quite content not socializing with other children and was often off in his own dream world. He was slow to do school work, and his fine-motor skills were under-developed with handwriting that looked like that of a preschooler. He also had difficulties making transitions and dealing with changes in routines.

His mom insisted for years that Nate had difficulties in certain areas and that he needed to be tested by the school psychologist. Finally, he was verified in fourth grade as a student with a learning disability in written expression. As fate would have it, I was his first resource teacher, having just graduated from college with a degree in special education. I figured out early on that Nate's immature handwriting was the least of his worries. While his standardized test scores were off the charts, he absolutely could not behave appropriately in social situations, particularly with peers. He was beginning to be avoided at best,

1

bullied at worst. Nate seemed to do things on purpose that would intentionally annoy or seem weird to his peers.

I had frank discussions with him on how his obsession with eating only one food resulting in serious gastric consequences, laughing during serious situations, and lecturing others forever in marine biology facts they had no interest in, were causing other kids not to like him. My talks seemed to go nowhere, as Nate retreated into his own world more and more.

After that year I married and moved out of town, only to see Nate once a year during family reunions. His mom would tell me how alienated he was from his peers, and she finally went back to school to get a degree in school psychology so she could learn herself and get her son the help he needed. About 10 years later, right before she died, my aunt told me that she had finally discovered the cause of Nate's problems. She said he was autistic. Autism was not my area of expertise, but I thought she must be mistaken because the autistic children I knew were nonverbal, visibly handicapped, and exhibited self-stimulating behavior. My cousin was none of these things. I filed my aunt's comment away in the back of my mind and continued my busy life.

Fast forward 10 years. I had moved out of state and was working as a special education teacher with middle and high school students with behavior disorders. Every day at about 1:00 in the afternoon, I would hear a seventh grader yelling, "I want it my way!" Then I'd hear things falling in the classroom as all the other students and their teacher quickly exited the room. I questioned the speech-language therapist who worked with the student, wondering why he wasn't in my behavioral program. (Ben soon became part of my caseload!) I learned he was diagnosed with Asperger Syndrome, a mild form of autism. He had difficulty with any type of change, had an obsession (area of special interest) in sports statistics, and was butting heads daily with the adults in charge.

I had an "aha" moment and suddenly made the connection between this child and my cousin Nate. Ben became my "guinea pig" as I began experimenting with teaching social skills to children who seemingly had none. One thing I learned early on was that 30 minutes of social skills class twice a week was not nearly enough, and that little transfer to real life took place. These students needed more social skills immersion than any one teacher with a full caseload could provide.

I looked around and realized an untapped resource in the form of the several hundred peers who surrounded my socially challenged students for hours daily. As time went on, I used these peers to help teach social skills to my socially challenged students, whether they were on the autism spectrum, had severe ADD, were English Language Learners, or had behavior disorders, using the Circle of Friends program outlined in this book. Implementing Learning Teams with the staff and involving my students in extracurricular activities further helped ensure that these kids had a positive school experience.

The Circle of Friends concept (Frederickson & Turner, 2001) is not new. It has been recommended by counselors and psychologists for quite some time. But as I started presenting workshops on teaching social skills to adolescents and mentioned using a Circle of Friends, I realized that the nuts and bolts of this concept were not widely known. I was inundated afterwards with emails and phone calls from parents, teachers, and administrators with questions on exactly how to implement a Circle of Friends. After typing long emails and spending hours on the phone, I decided a user-friendly program that busy school personnel could easily implement was needed. Hence this book came into being.

Unfortunately, my cousin Nate never received the social skills training he needed when he was a child. We just didn't have the knowledge then that we have now. He got his college degree in science, but never was able to turn it into a career. He has been working the graveyard shift at a bakery for the past 10 years, and lives a life of quiet solitude. On the bright side, Ben is a successful college student and an active member of the community and his church. Constant social readjustment and feedback is required as he moves through the different phases of his life, but he definitely had a happy, involved, emotionally satisfying experience in high school that served as a stepping stone to the adult world.

In this book you'll find step-by-step instructions for implementing a Circle of Friends, Learning Teams, and extracurricular activities for socially challenged students. There are also handouts to copy, scripts to use, and real-life situations you'll be able to relate to. Have fun as you introduce these ideas to the students and staff members in your life and acquaint them with the world of unique differences! And, a huge thank-you for all you do to improve the lives of children every day!

– M.S.

# CIRCLE BASICS

## Commonly Asked Questions

### So, just what is a Circle of Friends?

A Circle of Friends (COF) is a group of peer mentors who are good social role models, chosen to interact with a socially challenged student on a regular basis.

### Who is a Circle of Friends for?

Kids of any age who have difficulty making friends are good candidates for a COF.

### Are there benefits for the peer mentors chosen to be in the COF, as well as for the target child?

Certainly! Peer mentors develop understanding, empathy, and respect for the individual differences of others. In addition to feeling good about what they are doing as participants in a COF, students can earn community service credit and in the process add a welcome piece to their resumés for future college applications. Some participants even develop an ongoing interest in kids with special needs and end up exploring careers in this area.

### How do you choose students to be in the Circle with the target kids?

It's a good idea to get recommendations from the classroom teachers for names of students who are well liked and respected by their peers, confident, and not afraid to reach out to others. It's also a good idea to choose one or two kids who have interests similar to those of the target student. For example, if Johnny likes computer games, it would be great if one or two of the chosen kids had the same interest. Select students whom the target child comes in contact with in classes, lunch, etc., on a daily basis.

### How many students do you choose to be in the Circle?
Anywhere from 6-10 is usually a good number, in addition to the target child.

### How much does it cost to have a Circle of Friends?
Free or close to it! COF can be implemented using existing staff. The only budget items would be snacks for Circle meetings, but that would be optional.

### Who is responsible for implementing a Circle of Friends?
COFs have been successfully implemented by general education teachers, special education teachers, principals, paraprofessionals, speech language therapists, and coaches.

### How much time does a Circle of Friends take?
Circles can meet weekly or every other week to begin with. As time goes on and a strong Circle is developed, it is usually sufficient to meet once a month. Circle meeting time is approximately 20-30 minutes.

### Who comes to Circle meetings?
The target child comes to one meeting per month. The facilitator and peer participants attend all meetings (see below).

### What do you do at Circle meetings?
There are two kinds of Circle meetings: those attended by the target child and those he/she does not attend. At the latter, the COF kids are educated on the condition or life situation that causes the target student to behave in certain ways, practice ways to help develop that student's social skills, and are instructed on how to communicate to adults when there are problems or they need social feedback.

At meetings where all students attend, social activities are planned with food, games, and other fun activities designed for the all kids to feel comfortable with each other and have time to practice social skills with adult monitoring.

### In addition to attending meetings and interacting with the target student daily, are there other things COF kids do?

Yes! COF kids are the eyes and ears in place of adults in the locker room, hallways, cafeteria, on the bus – places where inappropriate social interactions are likely to take place. COF kids are instructed to tell adults when bullying takes place or when the arget child is behaving in socially inappropriate ways. This helps the adults be able to give immediate feedback to the student and provide relevant social skills training.

### Are parents involved in a Circle of Friends?

Parents are notified ahead of time that a recommendation has been made to start up a COF for their child. An explanation is given at that time of what a COF is and how it will be implemented. Parents of peer mentors invited to participate in a COF are also contacted.

### How does the target child feel about needing a COF?

Usually, the child knows he[1] has difficulty making friends and is appreciative, even if initially apprehensive. The student comes to look forward to Circle activities and is happy that he is gradually being more comfortable at school in social situations. But don't be surprised if initially the child is opposed to the idea, especially at the first few Circle social meetings. The child will be out of his comfort zone, and it may take a few meetings before he begins to embrace the concept. Be persistent, even if the child protests at first.

### How long do the kids chosen for a Circle remain in the Circle?

Some of the kids remain in the COF until the target child graduates. But there can be fluctuations. For example, you will need to switch out students and add new ones if you find a child is not participating or engaging the target child. Another time when you would add new kids to the Circle is when new classes are assigned or new activities offered where

---

[1] *Throughout the book we alternate the pronouns he and she.*

no Circle friends are present. This typically happens as a child progress through different grades in school.

As students enter their preteen and early teen years, friendships and interests often change. When students enter high school, they begin to choose specific interest-related activities to join. The facilitator should continue to monitor where the target child is throughout the day and assign new Circle friends as needed. For example, a freshman may choose to join the school's theatre group, working backstage to help design sets. At that point you would consider adding kids in theatre to the target child's Circle. If a new bus route becomes part of a child's school day, consider adding a student or two who ride the same bus.

# WHO CAN BENEFIT
# FROM A CIRCLE OF FRIENDS?

The following examples illustrate who you might consider forming a Circle of Friends for.

*James is a 7th grader with Asperger Syndrome, an autism spectrum disorder. He's a straight A student with incredible background knowledge in subjects ranging from aeronautics, Ancient Egyptian history and culture, to advanced algebra. But he has limited social skills and rarely interacts with peers. James picks his nose, chews pencils and paper obsessively, and gets angry when schedules change or things don't happen the way he thinks they should. He has extreme difficulty doing group projects, a common activity in the middle school curriculum. When other students try to talk to James, he frequently becomes rude, either ignoring them or telling them he doesn't have time for them.*

- **Students with autism spectrum disorders benefit from a Circle of Friends.**

*Mr. Jones, high school principal, seems to spend an inordinate portion of his day disciplining the same three boys over and over. They constantly disrupt classes and are rewarded by the attention they receive from the other students.*

- **Teachers and administrators can benefit from a Circle of Friends.**

*Miranda is a popular cheerleader and academic and social leader in her 9th-grade class. She always had a heart for "the underdog." She just tried to befriend a new girl, Tammi, who had recently been placed in a foster home in her school district. At first things seemed to go O.K., but lately Tammi has made some mean comments about cheerleaders being "stupid airheads" that bother Miranda. Miranda wants to reach out, but is angry with Tammi for her cruel comments.*

- **Non-socially challenged, empathetic students who have a desire to reach out to isolated students benefit from a Circle of Friends.**

*Jason is a good-looking 10th-grade boy with ADD. His difficulty focusing in class has made success in traditional academic subjects a rarity for him. So, although he is a talented wrestler, Jason often sits out meets since he is frequently on the fail list at school. Jason excels in car mechanics and construction classes, but often blurts out inappropriate comments to peers in an effort to get their attention. Although he had friends in grade school, he is rarely invited to the homes of those kids any more. He is starting to gain acceptance from the drug-using "party crowd" and is considering joining rather than living in isolation from his peers.*

- **Students with ADD and those who have lack of impulse control resulting in ostracism from the group can benefit from a Circle of Friends.**

*Courtney, a bright, pretty, but extremely overweight 6th grader recently moved into a foster home in the district. She tries to get attention by starting fights with her peers and freely discusses her history as an abuse victim. The other students are afraid of her and avoid her whenever possible.*

- **Students who come from dysfunctional families and lack basic social skills can benefit from a Circle of Friends.**

*Tom is a 10th grader with a reputation for being a bully. He has lately targeted two special education students on his bus, one of whom has autism and the other, mild mental retardation. He has been calling them names like "retard" and teaching them to say vulgar words they do not know the meaning of.*

- **Students who display bullying behavior can benefit from a Circle of Friends.**

*Maria is an ELL (English Language Learner) student, whose family recently moved to the United States from Guatemala. Maria speaks very limited English and was found crying in the girls' bathroom during lunch. Apparently, she is too overwhelmed and scared to walk into the cafeteria. She rarely interacts with anyone during the school day.*

- **ELL students and other students who feel isolated during the school day can benefit from a Circle of Friends.**

*Teachers in a local middle school have expressed concern about the number of cliques cropping up and the unusually cruel way students have been treating each other this year. They have spoken to their classes whenever the opportunity presented itself, but little seems to have changed.*

- **ALL students and staff can benefit from a Circle of Friends at some point or another.**

# GETTING STARTED

The following step-by-step guide simplifies the task of setting up a Circle of Friends.

- Call parents to explain what a Circle of Friends is and why you think their child would benefit. It may be preferable to contact the parents by phone instead of a letter due to the sensitive nature of the contact. A phone call allows parents the opportunity to immediately ask any questions they may have. A form letter is included on page 14 in case you choose to use a letter instead of a phone call, or desire to use both.

- Send a letter home to the parents of peer mentors who are invited to be in the Circle of Friends explaining what it is (see page 15).

- Speak to the target child, explaining in simple terms what a COF is and how it will work.

- Choose 6-10 students from the child's class to be in the Circle of Friends. Pick students who are in classes and extracurricular activities with the target child.

- Meet with the potential Circle kids (the target student does NOT attend this meeting) to explain the program and invite them to participate.

# Sample Letter to Parents of Target Child

Dear _____,

Your child has been identified as a student who may benefit from taking part in a Circle of Friends. A Circle of Friends consists of your child and peers who have been identified as good social role models. Kids in the Circle of Friends learn more about your child and are encouraged to get to know him/her better through daily conversations and lunch time spent together. The peers in your child's Circle of Friends are also taught to give social feedback to your child when needed. We also have monthly meetings for the purpose of socializing and getting to know each other better. The purpose of a Circle of Friends is to provide social skills immersion with peers on a daily basis and promote feelings of belonging in the school community.

If you have any questions, feel free to call or email me at: _____

Please sign below if you give permission for your child to be part of a Circle of Friends.

Sincerely,

. . . . . . . . . . . . . . . . . . . . . . . . . . . . . . . . . . . . . . . . . . . . . . . . . . . . . . . . . . . . . .

I give permission for my child to participate in a Circle of Friends at school.

_____
(parent signature)                                    (date)

# **Sample Letter to Parents of Peer Mentor**

Dear _____,

Your child has been identified as a good social role model and chosen to consider participating in a Circle of Friends for _____ (target child's name).*

A Circle of Friends is a group of peers who agree to interact with a student who has challenges learning social skills. Being in a Circle of Friends involves your son/daughter having daily conversations, periodically having lunch together, providing social skills feedback to the target student, communicating with the Circle facilitator, and meeting several times per month with the group members to share progress and brainstorm ideas on how to help _____ develop his/her social skills. A Circle of Friends is beneficial for both the target child and the other participants. The target student has the opportunity to interact with peers on a daily basis, practicing social skills while feeling accepted at school. At the same time, your child is able to be a good role model and learn about accepting individual differences.

This is a completely voluntary endeavor; feel free to discuss this with your child and call or email me at _____ if you have any questions. Please sign and return this form if you give permission for your child to participate in the Circle of Friends.

Thank you!

Sincerely,

· · · · · · · · · · · · · · · · · · · · · · · · · · · · · · · · · · · · · · · · · · · · · · · · · · · · · · · · · · · · · · · ·

I give permission for my child to participate in a Circle of Friends for _____

_____

(parent signature)                                                         (date)

*If for some reason, you don't think it is appropriate to mention the target child's name, substitute the following text: Your child has been identified as a good social role model and chosen to consider participating in a Circle of Friends for a child at school who needs opportunities to get to know other kids and socially interact with them during the school day.*

# SCRIPTS

The following are ideas for what to say when contacting parents and communicating with kids to introduce them to the Circle of Friends idea.

## To Parents:

"Hello, Mrs. Smith. As you know, I've been working with Darren on his social skills. I'd like to set up a Circle of Friends to give him a chance to interact more with his peers during the school day, and to give the other kids an opportunity to get to know him better. We'll choose 6-10 kids from his class and give instruction and time in school for them to get to know each other better. I think this will really help Darren make friends and feel more comfortable socially in school. Do you have any questions for me?"

## To Target Child:

"Hey, Charlie. I know we've talked about how you want to meet more kids at school and make more friends. I'd like to start up a Circle of Friends for you so we can help make that happen. A Circle of Friends is a group of kids who want to get to know you better and need to learn how to do that. Sometimes I'll have meetings with your Circle of Friends with you there, and sometimes without you there. Sometimes we'll even have lunch together, parties, and games. Are there any kids you'd like me to invite into your Circle?"

## To Circle Kids:

"Thanks for coming in to see me today. Do you all know Carrie? She's in some of your classes. Carrie would like to have more kids at school get to know her better. You might not know it, but she has _____ (Asperger Syndrome, Tourette Syndrome, is new at school and has moved around a lot, has trouble focusing, etc.), and that makes it challenging for her to make friends with kids her age. So, we're going to set up a Circle of Friends for her to help her with that. Your teachers have recommended you to be in Carrie's Circle because you're leaders in your class.

Being in Carrie's Circle of Friends will involve a few things. First of all, we'll meet for about 20-30 minutes every few weeks to talk about ways to interact with Carrie. Once a month or so we'll get together with Carrie to play games, have snacks, or a pizza lunch. If you choose to be in Carrie's Circle of Friends, you'll be asked to be a friendly face to her in school, have a conversation or two with her every day, and to eat lunch with her once every week or two. I don't want you to say yes to being in her Circle right now, but to go home and think about it tonight and let me know tomorrow if you're interested. If this isn't for you right now, that's fine. We need kids in her Circle who can make a commitment, so just get back to me and let me know either way. Thanks!"

# CIRCLE MEETINGS
*The Key to Communication*

In the following pages we will look at ways to successfully facilitate the cornerstone of Circle of Friends – the Circle meeting.

## Circle Meetings WITHOUT the Target Child in Attendance

### *Purpose?*

- To educate the Circle kids on the conditions/challenges of the target child.

- To provide a time for Circle kids to communicate on how things are going and answer specific questions they may have or difficulties they are experiencing interacting with the target child.

- To give them positive feedback on the job they're doing!

- To teach them specific strategies for interacting with the target child.

### *How Often?*

- Once every week or two for 20-30 minutes to start with works well. As time goes on and the Circle kids become more confident in their roles, you can drop back to every few weeks and eventually once a month.

### *When?*

- Whenever you can find the time. Some schools do lunch meetings where students bring their lunch, during homeroom, breaks and recess, before school, after school ... whenever it works. If "we can't spare the time" becomes an issue for teachers, remind them that taking time for a Circle pays "time dividends" in the form of an appropriately engaged child with fewer discipline problems and office referrals. Be sure to give the students a couple of days' notice, especially if you are pulling them from a study hall period, so they can plan ahead.

# Circle Meetings WITH the Target Child in Attendance

### *Purpose?*

- To provide structured time for all the kids in the Circle to interact, so the target child can practice social skills. Structured activities are recommended since socially challenged kids may have trouble integrating otherwise.

- To provide time for the kids to get to know each other better.

- To have fun.

### *How Often?*

- Every other week to once a month.

### *When?*

- Same as the other meetings, but these are often fun to do during lunch when it's more relaxed and can take place in a party-like atmosphere.

## Sample Circle Meeting Invitations

You're Invited

# Circle of Friends Meeting

For Danny Smith's Circle

When: Thursday, January 26, 11:30-11:50

Where: Room S-4

Special Note: You will be excused
from attending homeroom.

You're Invited

# Circle of Friends Meeting

For Tim Tegler's Circle

Where: Mr. Hagan's Room

When: During Homeroom Period, Feb. 2nd

Special Note: Please be on time and bring paper and pen.

You're Invited

# Circle of Friends Meeting

For Ashley Keel's Circle

When: Monday, Dec. 22, during lunch

Where: Mrs. Brown's Room

Special Note: Christmas party! Pizza will be served, so
don't bother bringing your lunch.

## Sample Circle Meeting Invitations

You're Invited
# Circle of Friends Meeting
For:
When:
Where:
Special Note:

You're Invited
# Circle of Friends Meeting
For:
When:
Where:
Special Note:

You're Invited
# Circle of Friends Meeting
For:
When:
Where:
Special Note:

# THE ART OF HAVING A CHAT

Carrying on meaningful conversations can be difficult for lots of people, but kids with so-cial challenges have an especially difficult time. However, the art of having conversations can be easily taught through both individual and group Circle activities. Teaching and practicing having a chat are important elements in any Circle of Friends. You'll need to teach it to all the Circle kids. After you learn about it, you might find yourself wishing the adults at your next party knew about it, too.

## How to change this scenario:
Student 1: "Hi."

Student 2: "Hi."

Student 1: "How're you?" (If you're lucky they'll get this far.)

Student 2: "Good."

Student 1: (After awkward pause) "O.K. Bye."

Student 2: "Bye."

## To this scenario:
Student 1: "Hi, Tom. How're you doing?"

Student 2: "Oh, hi Matt. I'm O.K. How about you?"

Student 1: "I'm O.K. What did you do last night?"

Student 2: "I got stuck going to my brother's hockey game. It was long and boring."

Student 1: "Don't you like hockey?"

Student 2: "No."

Student 1: "I don't like it either."

Student 2: "What did you do last night?"

Student 1: "I played my new video game."

Student 2: "What game is it?"

Student 1: "The new Tony Hawk game. It's really cool, and I'm already able to do through level four."

Student 2: "I have the first Tony Hawk game. It's an older one, but I really like it."

Student 1: "If you want to, maybe you could come to my house some time and play my new one."

Student 2: "Yeah, maybe I could. That would be good."

Student 1: "Well, the bell is going to ring soon, so I better go."

Student 2: "O.K., bye."

Student 1: "See ya."

# Step-by-Step Guide to Teaching How to Chat

You'll need to actively teach both the target child and the peers in the Circle of Friends how to have a chat. Most kids don't know how to do this naturally and, therefore, need both direct lessons and repeated practice.

## 1. Teaching the Target Child

At first, the target child should practice one on one with an adult when possible. This could take place before school, after school, during free time, or during resource or speech time if the child receives those services. Depending on the child's needs, you may need to practice this concept over a LONG period of time.

**Example:**

*   "Mark, the kids in your Circle of Friends want to get to know you better, and the best way to do this is to have conversations or chats with you. We're going to practice how to have a chat with other kids for a few minutes during our resource/ speech time until it's easy for you to do …"

## 2. Teaching Participating Peers

Participating peers will need to be taught how to chat informally at one of your earliest Circle meetings. Don't underestimate their need for continued review of this, too. Role-playing is a great way to teach this concept, and Circle meetings provide a perfect vehicle.

**Example:**

*   "Today during our Circle of Friends meeting, we're going to practice how to have chats. Carrie will have difficulty for a while starting and keeping a conversation going, so I need to make sure you know how to do it so you can lead her along until she knows how to do it herself."

## 3. Using Chat Charts and Reinforcers

Target children may be resistant to engaging in conversations. Remember that having appropriate, two-way chats is probably not a strength for them. As a result, they may be uncomfortable, especially at the beginning.

Having target students keep track of their conversations using a chat chart (see page 34) provides visual feedback, which is important for them as many are visual learners. In addition, you may need to provide some system of reinforcement. For example, if verbal praise is not enough, you could give something tangible such as special note paper, computer time, or something else you know they would like. You will also have to determine how often they need the reinforcement; some kids are able to wait until their entire chart is filled up before they get a reinforcer, whereas others may need a reinforcer after just a few conversations in the beginning. As they get repeated practice and become more comfortable having chats with peers, you will not need to use anything to get them to do this. With or without a tangible reinforcer, the chat chart is a great tool to ensure enough practice is taking place on an ongoing basis.

**Example:**

- "Danielle, now that you know how to have a chat with other kids, I'm going to ask that you have at least two chats a day. I would like you to write on this chat chart every time you have one. I know this might be hard for you at first and you've told me you don't want to do it, so when you have filled out your chat chart for an entire week, I'm going to let you choose a special notebook or note paper or pencil from this box."

- "Zach, when your chat chart is filled for the week, you'll get 15 extra minutes of free time on the computer."

## 4. Teaching Chat Vocabulary Words

Teach the following chat vocabulary words to both the target child and the peer mentors: *chat starter, chat topics, ask-backs*, and *chat ending*. You will use these words over and over again when you teach kids how to have a chat.

**Example:**

- "Let's review the chat vocabulary words we learned at our last Circle meeting. List as many chat topics as you can remember. Great!  Next, what do we call it when you answer a question someone asks you and then you ask them the same question about them? Yes! An ask-back. Now, let's practice doing an ask-back in a conversation. Joel and Katie, let's have you come up and start. Which chat topic do you want to choose?"

## 5. Planning Chats Ahead of Time

Target kids who really struggle will need you to help them plan their conversations before they actually engage peers.

### Example:

- "Abbie, where would you like to have your first chat today? How about in a few minutes in the cafeteria when you get breakfast? Who could you look for to talk with? Take a look at the chat topic list and choose a topic to chat with Marcie about. Good luck! Let me know how it goes, and don't forget to fill out your chart when you come in for study hall later this morning."

  Afterwards when you see the child again, follow up: "Hi Abbie! How did your chat go today? Who did you talk to? What was your chat topic? Did you remember to do an ask-back? What did Marcie talk about? It sounds like you did a great job! How about filling out your conversation chart now?"

## 6. Monitoring Chats

Especially in the beginning, you will need to monitor chats while instruction is taking place by listening in, encouraging, and providing feedback when necessary. Use Circle of Friends kids to do this with, as well as other adults who interact with the target child on a daily basis.

### Example:

- "How about doing an ask-back now?" "Jake, you've been doing all the talking, and it looks like Sarah is getting bored. How about asking her a question now?"

- "Go ahead Danny, say your chat starter now."

- "Sounds like you're just about done. How about using a chat ending now?"

# Having a Chat

The following are the concrete steps of starting, maintaining, and ending a chat that need to be taught directly followed by practice.

## Step 1: Chat Starters

It's important to start a chat with a greeting, like saying "hi" and the person's name. When you say the person's name, it makes her feel important or special and tells her that you like her.

## Some examples:

- "Hi, Ben."
- "Hello, Mrs. Kanes."
- "What's up, Marissa?"
- "Hey, Tom. How's it going?"

## Step 2: Choose a Chat Topic

If it's hard to think of what to talk about, choose from the topic list.

(Provide list on page 35 or more customized list that you put together yourself.)

## Step 3: Making Small Talk

Small talk is when you talk about things that interest you and the other person. This is the main part of the conversation. Some things to remember:

- When you don't know what to talk about, choose something from the topic list.

- Show interest in the other person by using ask-backs. An ask-back is when you answer a question someone asks you and then you ask the same question, too. Remember, a conversation is not all about you.

- If you start with one topic of conversation, often it will lead to other topics, and that's O.K.

### Ask-Backs

Hi, Maggie. What are you doing this weekend?

Hi, Emily. I'm going to visit my grandmother and ride her horse if I'm lucky. What are you going to do this weekend?

I'm going to the movies with my mom. It must be fun to ride a horse. What kind of horse is it?

Ask-backs show you are interested in the other person.

## Step 4: Keeping the Chat Going

Are you afraid the conversation will end before you want it to? Just remember, one thing will lead to another if you just keep doing ask-backs and asking questions!

**Example:**

Tom:  Hi, Ben. Man! It's really cold out today!

Ben:  Hi, Tom. Yeah, it's freezing! It took forever for the bus to get to my house this morning. I thought I'd get frostbite! Did you have to wait long for the bus this morning?

Tom:  I don't take the bus. My sister has her diver's license, so she drives me.

Ben:  You're really lucky that you don't have to take the bus.

Tom:  Well, sometimes I don't feel lucky riding with her. Since it's her car, we have to listen to her music all the time and I don't like it.

Ben:  What kind of music does she like?

Tom:  She likes country music, and I can't stand it. I like rock and nothing but rock. What kind of music do you like?

Ben:  I like rock, too. I have a guitar and I'm learning to play, but it's pretty hard. I can play a few songs now though.

Tom:  That's really cool. I'd like to learn to play the guitar, but I've always taken saxophone lessons.

Ben:  Do you play in the school band?

Tom:  Yeah, we're playing at the basketball game tonight. Are you going?

Ben:  I'm not sure. I might go. Maybe I'll see you there?

Tom:  O.K. Maybe I'll see you tonight at the game. Bye.

Ben:  Bye.

Simply by asking questions, this conversation expanded and became more meaningful:

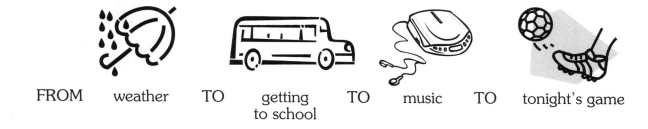

FROM    weather    TO    getting to school    TO    music    TO    tonight's game

## Step 5: Chat Endings

It's easy to end a chat smoothly. Just do the following:

1. Say something that gives the other person a clue that you have to end the conversation.
   - "Well, the bell is going to ring."
   - "Looks like class is going to start soon."
   - "My mom will be here soon to pick me up."
   - "Well, I better get started on my homework."
   - "Looks like it's time to go."
   - "I need to be going now."
   - "I better be getting to the cafeteria."

2. Give a goodbye.
   - "See ya."
   - "Goodbye."
   - "Bye."
   - "I'll be seeing you."
   - "See you later."

## **Chat Chart**

Fill out a square for each chat you have with Circle friends and other kids this week.

Next to "Who?" write the name of who you talked with, next to "Topic?" write which topic you talked about, and next to "Ask-Backs?" write "yes" if you remembered to do an ask-back.

| Monday | Tuesday | Wednesday | Thursday | Friday |
|---|---|---|---|---|
| Who?<br><br>Topic?<br><br>Ask-Backs? | Who?<br><br>Topic?<br><br>Ask-Backs? | Who?<br><br>Topic?<br><br>Ask-Backs? | Who?<br><br>Topic?<br><br>Ask-Backs? | Who?<br><br>Topic?<br><br>Ask-Backs? |
| Who?<br><br>Topic?<br><br>Ask-Backs? | Who?<br><br>Topic?<br><br>Ask-Backs? | Who?<br><br>Topic?<br><br>Ask-Backs? | Who?<br><br>Topic?<br><br>Ask-Backs? | Who?<br><br>Topic?<br><br>Ask-Backs? |
| Who?<br><br>Topic?<br><br>Ask-Backs? | Who?<br><br>Topic?<br><br>Ask-Backs? | Who?<br><br>Topic?<br><br>Ask-Backs? | Who?<br><br>Topic?<br><br>Ask-Backs? | Who?<br><br>Topic?<br><br>Ask-Backs? |
| Who?<br><br>Topic?<br><br>Ask-Backs? | Who?<br><br>Topic?<br><br>Ask-Backs? | Who?<br><br>Topic?<br><br>Ask-Backs? | Who?<br><br>Topic?<br><br>Ask-Backs? | Who?<br><br>Topic?<br><br>Ask-Backs? |
| Who?<br><br>Topic?<br><br>Ask-Backs? | Who?<br><br>Topic?<br><br>Ask-Backs? | Who?<br><br>Topic?<br><br>Ask-Backs? | Who?<br><br>Topic?<br><br>Ask-Backs? | Who?<br><br>Topic?<br><br>Ask-Backs? |

Name: _____Date:_____

My goal is to have (#)_____ conversations this week.

## Chat Topic List

Things you can talk about with anyone.

Music

Sports

Weather

TV

School

Movies

Your Day/ Weekend

Books

Current Activity

Pets

Family

Hobbies

# CIRCLE GAMES AND ACTIVITIES

The following games have been chosen due to their noncompetitive nature. The purpose of Circle activities is to provide a safe, fun environment for the students to get to know one another better and to provide time for social skills practice. Search the Internet, books, and other resources for more options if desired.

Possible websites include:

http://kimscorner4teachertalk.com

http://sdces.sdstate.edu/cld/files/ice%20breaker%20ideas.pdf

http://www.educationworld.com

http://www.cplrmh.com/icebreakers.html

http://midhudson.org/program/ideas/Icebreaker_Activities_Kids.rtf

When choosing meeting activities, always remember they are to be comfortable, positive experiences for the target child. Use your knowledge of his strengths and areas of challenge to avoid or modify activities so he can be successful. For example, choose activities that do not involve touching if the child has tactile issues. Kids with reading difficulties should use materials that either do not involve reading, or that are written at their independent reading level (other options include use of tape recorders, etc.). Similarly, if writing is a challenge, choose activities that require limited writing, or none at all (depending on the child's challenges, access to a computer or other electronic device may be another option). On the other hand, if an activity "showcases" a particular child's strength, by all means, go for it!

**Data Processing** – Tell kids they are to collect "data" to "process" by making lists of the following: alphabetical list of class by last names, alphabetical on each other according to favorite food, length of hair from shortest to longest, shoe size from smallest to largest, birthdays from beginning of the year to the end, number of letters in last names from smallest to largest, length of thumbs from shortest to longest.

**Name Tag Maker** – Give each group member a 5 x 7 card for a name tag. Give these directions: (1) Put your name in the center of your card; (2) In the upper-left corner, write four things that you like to do; (3) In the upper-right corner, write your favorite singers or groups; (4) In the lower-left corner, write your four favorite movies; and (5) In the lower-right corner, write four adjectives that describe you.

When everyone has finished, have them mingle with the group for a few minutes. Without talking, they are to read the upper-left corner of the other group members' cards. When time is up, they are to find one or two people who are most like them and visit with them for a few minutes. When time is up, they are to mingle again, this time reading the upper-right corner of the others group members' cards. Again, they are to find the one or two people most like them and visit. Repeat with the lower-left corner and lower-right corner information.

**Birthday Line** – Explain to the group that this is a nonverbal exercise. Without talking, the group is to form a single line around the room according to birthdays. For example, people with January birthdays will be at the beginning of the line, earliest January dates first, followed in order by later dates. The line progresses by months and days, with December birthdays at the end. Persons with the same birthday share the same space in line. They must communicate nonverbally (no lip reading or finger spelling allowed) using gestures. When the line is completed, each person will say his or her birthday beginning with January.

**Height Line** – Ask the students to close their eyes. Without opening their eyes, students are asked to arrange themselves by height in a straight line. They may arrange by feeling the height or saying their height out loud. The only restriction is that they are not to open their eyes.

**Having a Chat** – Teach kids how to have a chat, role-playing different scenarios. Be sure to teach how to keep the conversation going using ask-backs. Students may need a lot of coaching at first, and you may need to jump in to make suggestions on how to keep it going.

**Relationship Circles** – Discuss Relationship Circles (see page 67) and have kids fill out a blank form, writing in the names of the people in their own Relationship Circles. Discuss the different ways they act with each circle level.

**Who Am I?** – Pin a card on each player's back with the name of a well-known couple or pair. It might be stars like Superman and Lois Lane, Batman and Robin; or combinations like cheese and crackers, tea and coffee, burgers and fries, etc. Each student must find out who he or she is by asking appropriate questions. Students are not allowed to directly ask "Who am I?" Only yes and no answers are allowed.

**Concentration** – Cover a tray of at least 12 assorted objects with a piece of cloth. When everyone is ready, uncover the tray for about 10 seconds and cover it or put it out of sight immediately. Everyone has to write down as many objects as they can remember. Uncover the tray and see how everyone did.

**Scary Story** – Have everyone sit in a circle. Tell the players that the object of this game is for the group to create a scary (funny, or dramatic) story. Have one person begin with "Once upon a time," or "One dark night …" The student continues until you clap your hands. Then the next person continues the story. The results are usually quite hilarious.

**TV Interview** – Pair students up and have them interview each other, asking what they watched on TV the night before and what the shows were about. Afterwards, students take turns telling the group about the shows they learned about.

**Describe Me** – Ask the kids to introduce themselves using two adjectives, one of which starts with the first letter of their first name, and the second with the first letter of their last name.

**Comic Strip Chaos** – Cut up comic strip frames and put them in a large container. Each participant takes a turn picking a comic strip frame and searches for others in the group who have the same comic strip sequence. When they have found everyone with the same strip, they have to arrange themselves so that the sequence of frames is in chronological order to form the actual comic strip.

**Riddles** – Have students make up riddles like the following. If the riddle is guessed on just the first clue, they get 10 points. If it's guessed on the second, they get 9 points, on the third 8 points, etc. The goal is to get the highest score possible.

**Riddle #1:**

I am not a bird, but I can fly.

I eat bugs and fruit.

I have fur.

I live in caves.

(bat)

**Riddle #2**

I'm white and round.

I'm the same size as an orange.

I'm hard; can't be eaten.

You hit me with a bat.

(baseball)

**Riddle #3:**

I'm a sport.

You need protective gear.

Each player uses a long, metal instrument.

Two people play in each match.

(fencing)

**Riddle #4:**

I am an animal.

I live in the sea.

I have poison stingers.

I have tentacles.

(jellyfish)

**Riddle #5:**

I am a food.

I am usually round.

I am cut into slices.

I have sauce and cheese.

(pizza)

**Riddle #6:**

I am a holiday.

There is usually no school this day.

A famous man,

Civil Rights Leader.

(Martin Luther King Day)

Kids also enjoy making up their own riddles to play this game.

**What's My Hobby?** – Have the students take turns acting out their favorite hobbies, foods, vacation spots, etc., while others take turns guessing what they are.

**Telephone Line** – Kids stand or sit in a line. The first person tells what kinds of job he/she would like to do some day and why. The next person repeats what the first person said and adds information about him/herself. The third person repeats what the first and second people say and adds his/her information. This continues through the line until the last person has to remember what everyone in the group has said.

**Getting-to-Know-You Bingo** (see pages 42-43)

Directions to students: Talk to people, crossing out squares when you find someone whom it applies to. You have "BINGO" when you get five across, up and down, or diagonally. Afterwards, share your card with the group by telling interesting things you learned about others.

# GETTING-TO-KNOW-YOU BINGO (SAMPLE COMPLETED BOARD)

| | | | |
|---|---|---|---|
| Mark here if you have ever traveled out of the state. Where? | Mark here if you have taken some kind of class outside of your regular school day. What was it? | Mark here if you can find someone to tell you what his or her dream job would be. What is it? | Mark here if you can find someone who has ever tried an extreme sport. What was it? |
| Mark here if you can find someone who is going into the same career field as you. What is it? | Mark here if you can find someone who did volunteer work last year. What did they do? | Mark here if you can find someone with more than two brothers and sisters. How many do they have? | Mark here if you can find someone who has traveled outside of the United States. Where was it? |
| Mark here if you find someone who has a paying job outside of school. Where? | Mark here if you find someone who has ever gone camping. Where? | Mark here if you can find someone who is certain he knows what he wants to do after high school? What? | Mark here if you get someone to give you a description of a car she would like to own. |
| Mark here if you are willing to share your biggest accomplishment with the group. | Mark here if you can find someone who has ever been in an accident. What happened? | Mark here if you can find someone to share her phobia with you. | Mark here if you can find someone who has an unusual hobby. What is it? |
| Mark here if you are willing to share a practical joke someone has played on you. | Mark here if you can find someone who has performed in public this year. Where? | Mark here if you can find someone who likes to eat an unusual food combination. What is it? | Mark here if you are willing to share your most embarrassing moment with the group. |
| | | | Mark here if you can find someone who has had to spend the night in the hospital recently. What happened to them? |
| | | | Mark here if you can find someone who has traveled on a plane. Where did they go? |
| | | | Mark here if you can get someone to tell you what her dream vacation would be. What is it? |

42

**GETTING-TO-KNOW-YOU BINGO (BLANK BOARD)**

| | | | | |
|---|---|---|---|---|
| | | | | |
| | | | | |
| | | | | |
| | | | | |
| | | | | |

# BOOK CLUBS

Book clubs are great Circle meeting activities for developing bonding, learning about individual differences, discussing peer social issues, and discovering ways to relate to each other. Students are asked to read the book before the Circle meeting, and the meeting time is used for discussion.

The books below have been selected because their content deals with social pressures, bullying, and individual differences. Questions/topics that can be explored include:

- What are the difficulties facing the characters?
- Have you ever been in a similar situation?
- How would you feel if _____ happened to you?
- What could you do in a similar situation?
- Is this something that happens here at school?
- Can you relate to this situation?
- Do you think_____ (target child) feels this way sometimes?
- How could you help him/her?

Read the book yourself before introducing it to make sure you are comfortable with the content and know it is appropriate for the students who will be participating in the book club.

## Recommend Titles

### *There's a Boy in the Girls' Bathroom* by Louis Sachar

Interest Level: 3-6, Reading Level: 5.0

Bradley Chalkers could care less about school, has no friends, and is obnoxious most of the time, even though he comes from a caring home. A new boy at school wants to become friends with Bradley and shows persistence in helping him change his ways.

### *Jackson Whole Wyoming* by Joan Clark

Interest Level: 5-8, Reading Level: 4.8

Tyler befriends Jackson, who has Asperger Syndrome, which affects his life as a middle school student.

### *Monkey* by Veronica Bennett

Interest Level: Young Adult

Harry must overcome his fears while dealing with the people in his life who bully him.

### *Loser* by Jerry Spinelli

Interest Level: 3-7, Reading Level: 5.2

This story is about a boy labeled a loser because he is clumsy, sloppy, and generally clueless. Kids reading this can relate to someone very different, yet very ordinary at the same time.

### *Freak the Mighty* by Rodman Philbrick

Interest Level: 5-8, Reading Level: 6.3

A mentally challenged hulk of a boy with a difficult home life befriends a brilliant boy with a physical disability, and the two team up to become unlikely friends. Together they become a formidable force helping each other in ways they never imagined possible.

### *Princess Ashley* by Richard Peck

Interest Level: Young Adult, Reading Level: 6.0

Chelsea, an ordinary girl trying to fit in at a new school, ignores her mother's disapproval of the clique of rich girls she is trying to join. A senseless tragedy helps Chelsea understand the true meaning of friendship.

### *The View From Saturday* by E. L. Konigsburg

Interest Level: 3-6, Reading Level: 4.8

Four 6th-grade quiz bowl champs and their paraplegic coach/teacher share stories of the challenges in their lives as they band together in a group called "The Souls."

### *Lizard* by Dennis Covington

Interest Level: Young Adult

Lucius Sims is treated poorly just because he is different. He is put into a home for boys with developmental disabilities even though he does not belong, and escapes in an adventure to find his freedom.

### *Geeks* by Jon Katz

Interest Level: Young Adult

This is a true story of two teens who learn to embrace their "geekiness" and develop promising futures while dealing with alienation in high school.

### *Hello, My Name Is Scrambled Eggs* by Jamie Gilson

Interest Level: 3-6, Reading Level: 4.6

This book describes the experiences (often humorous) of an immigrant family trying to learn a new culture. Prejudice, stereotyping, and difficulties assimilating to a new culture are explored.

### *Kissing Doorknobs* by Terry Spencer Hesser

Interest Level: Young Adults

This is a story of a girl with obsessive compulsive disorder who is befriended by a boy with the same problem. They fight their OCD while finding acceptance among family and friends.

### *The Wish* by Gail Carson Levine

Interest Level: 5-8, Reading Level: 4.8

Wilma, an unpopular girl, meets a fairy who grants her one wish, which she uses to become popular. Valuable lessons are learned along the way.

### *Stuck in Neutral* by Terry Trueman

Interest Level: 5-12, Reading Level: 6.7

This book relates the thoughts and feelings of a boy who is crippled and cannot communicate with anyone. The book shows the effects on families who have members with disabilities.

### *Memories of Summer* by Ruth White

Interest Level: 5-8, Reading Level: 5.2

A family has to learn to deal with an older sibling diagnosed with schizophrenia.

### *The Curious Incident of the Dog in the Night-Time* by Mark Haddon

Interest Level: Adult

The adventures of a 15-year-old boy with autism bring the reader directly into the mind of a teenager with this condition in this humorous, touching story.

### *When Zachary Beaver Came to Town* by Kimberly Willis

Interest Level: 5-8, Reading Level: 5.0

When a 643-pound boy comes to town, the main characters, Toby and Cal, learn to deal with complicated subjects such as accepting differences, divorce, the Vietnam War, and friendship.

### *Double Dutch* by Sharon M. Draper

Interest Level: 5-8, Reading Level: 5.3

Two middle school-aged friends keep secrets (one cannot read and the other's father has been missing for weeks) that could have devastating effects on their futures.

### *Stargirl* by Jerry Spinelli

Interest Level: 5-10, Reading Level: 6.1

After being home-schooled most of her life, Stargirl enters Mica High School in the 10th grade. Stargirl, who is not afraid to be different, is a happy girl concerned with the feelings of others, despite attempts to make her conform.

### *A Different Life* by Lois Keith

Interest Level: Young Adult

When 15-year-old Libby gets a bad infection, she must struggle with the long road to recovery and the possibility that she may never walk again.

### *Figuring out Francis* by Gina Willner-Pardo

Interest Level: 5-8, Reading Level: 5.0

A young girl struggles with changing friendships when a close friend no longer wants to associate with her. At the same time, she has to deal with the difficulties of having a grandmother with Alzheimer's.

### *Running on Dreams* by Herb Heiman

Interest Level: Young Adult

As Justin, a 15-year-old boy with autism, starts his first semester mainstreamed in regular middle school, he is teamed up with "buddy" Brad, the popular, school track star. Both boys deal with teenage issues as they learn to understand each other.

### *Ann Drew Jackson* by Joan Clark

Interest Level: 5-8, Reading Level: 4.8

*Ann Drew Jackson* brings to light a truth that teachers have known for years – occasionally kids who have to deal with issues that are out of their control, such as Jackson Thomas, a fifth-grade boy with Asperger Syndrome, can become a guiding light for their peers. Jackson helps Hillary Branson, another fifth grader, in a profound way, primarily by being himself – something Hillary has difficulty with. Through the experiences of Jackson and Hillary, readers learn that people are people despite life's circumstances.

## Book Club Study Guide Questions

To get you started, here you'll find study guide questions to use with your students on three books: *Joey Pigza Swallowed the Key* by Jack Gantos (ADD), *There's a Boy in the Girl's Bathroom* by Louis Sachar (Behavior Disorders), and *Jackson Whole Wyoming* by Joan Clark (Asperger Syndrome). It is recommended you have your students read a portion of the book you choose ahead of time, and then use the discussion questions as a springboard for helping them understand their Circle friend. You may also be able to find study guide questions on other books by doing an Internet search. Some of these may be printed and used for free; for others there is a fee. Two sites that have study guides are Ellen's Teaching Made Easier by Ellen Gabor (http://www.e-tme.com) and Mary Schlieder's Schools with Open Arms (http://schoolswithopenarms.com).

## *There's a Boy in The Girl's Bathroom* by Louis Sachar
## Book Club Discussion Questions for Students
## Topic: Behavioral Problems

**Chapter 1:**

What kind of a student was Bradley Chalkers? How do his classmates feel about him? How do you know? How does his teacher feel about him? How do you know? Do you think it was right for Mrs. Ebbel to say, "Well ... nobody likes to sit ... there"? Why or why not? Do you think it was strange for Bradley to tell Jeff to give him a dollar or he'd spit on him? Why?

**Chapter 2:**

What is your definition of a bully? Do you think Bradley is a bully? Why or why not? Why do you think he lies? What do you think it means that as long as Bradley hated the other kids, it didn't matter what they thought of him? Why does Jeff's behavior confuse him?

**Chapter 3:**

Why do you think Bradley enjoys playing so much in the world of his little animals? Does he want other people to know he does this? Why? Have you ever had to hide something you like because you thought other people might make fun of you? Bradley lies about his mother's promise to take him to the zoo. Why do you think that is? Do you think it's fair that he got in trouble at the dinner table?

**Chapter 4:**

The new school counselor says she can't wait to meet Bradley. Why do you think this is so?

**Chapter 5:**

What does Jeff do to try to be friends with Bradley? Why do you think Jeff wants to be friends with Bradley? Why do you think Bradley treats Jeff the way he does? Have you ever been a new student? What was it like? Can you think of ways to make things at school easier for new kids?

**Chapter 6:**

What happens to Jeff when he is confused about where to find the counselor's office? How do you think he feels? Have you ever had a really embarrassing moment? Do you want to share what it was?

**Chapter 7:**

Do you think Jeff likes his nickname? Have you ever called a classmate a nickname or been called one yourself? Is there anything you can do about being called mean nicknames?

How do you think Jeff feels about the way his teacher said out loud that nobody likes to sit near Bradley? Do you think his teacher should have said that? Why or why not?

What does it mean to be "smiling on the outside, but not smiling on the inside"? Have you ever done that? When? Why?

Carla and Jeff talk about the definition of a friend. What is your definition of a friend? Do you think it's true that if Jeff is friendly to Bradley, then Bradley will be friendly back? Do you think this will happen right away? Why or why not?

**Chapter 8:**

Why do you think Bradley pretends he doesn't want to eat lunch with Jeff? What does Bradley say to Melinda that is inappropriate? What would you do if someone threatened you or another student?

**Chapter 9:**

Why do you think Bradley talks to Carla the way he does? Does she seem to like him? Why do you think she acts like she believes everything he says? Do you think she really does believe him? If not, what do you think she's trying to do?

**Chapter 10:**

Jeff tells Bradley to try some basic social skills. What are they? How can kids like Bradley learn these simple things? Is there something you can do to help kids learn social skills who don't know them?

**Chapter 11:**

Why do you think Jeff keeps making excuses to not do the things Bradley wants him to do? Have you ever had other kids try to get you to do things you didn't want to do? How did you handle it? How could you handle it in the future?

**Chapter 12:**

Colleen is having a problem knowing who to invite to her birthday party. Have you ever had this problem? How did you handle it? Have your feelings ever been hurt by not being invited somewhere?

**Chapter 13:**

Bradley wants to keep Jeff to himself as his friend. Why do you think this is? What do you think will happen if Jeff makes other friends? Has this ever happened to you?

**Chapter 14:**

Lori started a fight by saying, "E-uuu, Bradley Chalkers," and then making a face. Is there another way Bradley could have handled it instead of fighting back? If you were ever in a situation like this, what could you do?

**Chapter 15:**

Why do you think Bradley blames the fight on Jeff?

**Chapter 16:**

Bradley's dad says the only reason bullies pick on kids is because the kids they pick on are afraid of them. Do you agree? Why do you think bullies pick on kids? What can you do when you're being bullied? What can you do if you see someone else being bullied? Is it always O.K. to tell on someone who's a bully? Why or why not?

**Chapter 17:**

Why do you think Jeff let the boys believe he was the one to give Bradley a black eye when he didn't? What do you think will happen to Bradley and Jeff's friendship?

**Chapter 18:**

Jeff now treats Bradley mean like the other boys do. Why do you think he turns on him like that? How do you think Bradley feels?

**Chapters 19-20:**

Jeff tells Carla he won't be in to see her any more because he now has friends and, besides, everyone will think he's weird if he has to go and talk to a counselor. Do you think someone is weird if they need to get special help from a counselor or resource teacher? Why or why not?

**Chapter 21:**

Carla tells Bradley that maybe the reason he doesn't like anybody is that he doesn't like himself. Do you agree with this? Do you know anyone who feels this way? Is there anything you can to for someone who doesn't act like they like themselves?

Bradley says he wants to fail. Do you believe him? Carla says the only reason Bradley says he wants to fail is that he's afraid he might fail if he tries. Have you ever been afraid to try something that you were afraid you might fail if you tried? What advice would you give Bradley?

**Chapter 22:**

Claudia told Bradley that Carla, the counselor, only liked him because it was her job to act like she liked him and that she really didn't. Do you agree? What do you think of the way Claudia treated her brother?

**Chapter 23:**

Carla says that if someone keeps saying bad things about someone or calling him bad names like "monster," the person eventually ends up believing it and acting like it. Do you agree with this? Do you know someone who is called bad names all the time who might start to believe it? Are you able to see the good in people that other people call "monsters"?

**Chapter 24:**

What went wrong with Colleen's communication with Jeff?

**Chapter 25:**

Why do you think Jeff lied about where he got his black eye? Have you ever done something wrong to fit in with a certain group of kids?

**Chapter 26:**

Bradley is being bullied and has to use the girls' bathroom as a place to hide so he doesn't get beat up. Have you ever been in a situation like this? Do you know someone who has? Where can kids go for help when they are being bullied?

**Chapters 27-28:**

Bradley has a long, bad habit of not doing his homework, and he thinks it's going to be really hard to change that. Do you have suggestions for how Bradley can turn things around? How could Carla help him? Do you know kids who get help with school work? Do you think that's fair?

**Chapters 29-31:**

Why do you think Bradley tore up his homework paper? What is he afraid of?

**Chapters 32-35:**

Even though Bradley knows some of the answers to the questions the teacher asks, he's too afraid to raise his hand to answer them. Have you ever felt that way? Do you think there are kids in your class who are afraid to answer, even if they are smart?

Jeff's friends encouraged him to beat up Bradley, but Jeff did the right thing. Do you think that took a lot of courage on Jeff's part? Do you think you would be able to stand up in front of a group and do the right thing?

**Chapter 36:**

Carla is surprised when Bradley asks her, "So, what's new?" Why? Do you remember to ask about the other person?

Bradley tells Carla he's never been to a real birthday party before. Do you think there are kids in your class who've never been invited to a birthday party? Do you think it bothers them?

**Chapter 37:**

Some parents want to get rid of the school counselor. Do you think schools need counselors? Why? Do you think it's O.K. for a kid to go talk to a counselor?

**Chapters 38-42:**

Bradley has a "meltdown" when he finds out Carla has to leave his school. Is it understandable that he would be upset? Have you ever seen other classmates "melt down"? Is there anything you can do to help them when this happens?

**Chapters 43-47:**

Bradley is very nervous about going to Colleen's birthday party? Why? Sometimes new experiences cause people to behave in strange ways. Has this ever happened to you or someone you know?

Jeff and the girls help Bradley understand how a birthday party works, so he won't be so nervous. Are there times at school when you could help someone understand something so they might not be so nervous?

In this book, kids started to be nice to Bradley, and when that happened, Bradley started to change. When Jeff acted friendly to him, when the boys let him play basketball with them, and when Colleen invited him to her birthday party, Bradley started to behave better. Do you know kids in your class who have trouble behaving? Are there things you can think of that you could do to help kids who are having problems behave better? What would some of those things be?

## *Joey Pigza Swallowed the Key* by Jack Gantos
## Book Club Discussion Questions for Students
## Topic: ADD

**Chapter 1:**

Joey has ADD. ADD stands for attention deficit disorder. This is another way of saying someone isn't able to pay attention in school or control themselves sometimes. Joey's medication works in the morning to help keep him calmed down, but when it wears off, he runs into trouble. What did he do to get into trouble? Do you have any classmates who behave like Joey sometimes? What did the teacher do to help Joey and the class?

**Chapter 2:**

Did you know that ADD can run in families? This means that if a kid has ADD, chances are he has a relative or more than one relative who has it, too. Who else in Joey's family do you think might have it?

If they had ADD as a kid, it often doesn't go away just because they grow up. What things does Joey's grandma do that show she may have ADD, too?

**Chapter 3:**

Do you think it was fair that Joey got to do jobs for Mrs. Maxy instead of having to do the President worksheet? Why or why not? Why do you think Mrs. Maxy let him do jobs instead?

Do you think Joey will be able to follow Mrs. Maxy's rules? Why or why not? Do you think he wants to follow the rules?

Joey says kids have called him names like Zippy because of the way he behaves. Do you think Joey likes this? Have you ever called someone names or been called names yourself? Can you think of some things the kids in Joey's class could do to help him instead of calling him names?

Was Joey happy that he ruined the chair at the pharmacy? How do you know? Do you think he likes doing bad things?

**Chapter 4:**

How was Joey bullied in the beginning of the chapter? What would you have done if you were there?

Every school has special education classes. What do kids think about kids who get special education services? What names do they call kids who go to special education? How do you think that makes them feel? Do you know what goes on in special education programs? (This is a good time to discuss with students the fact that everyone has challenges. It's just that some are more obvious than others.) What are some of the things you're good at? What are some things you're not good at? Even though Joey goes to special ed., do you think he's smart? In what ways does he show that he's smart?

**Chapter 5:**

Why do you think Joey swallowed the key a second time? Have you or your classmates ever tried to get someone to do things they shouldn't? Is there anything you could have done if you had been in class to stop Joey from swallowing the key?

How are Joey's good days different from his bad days? How are your good days different from your bad days?

**Chapter 6:**

How did Joey feel when his teacher wouldn't let him eat the pie or use a knife to carve a pumpkin? Do you think this was fair? Is it necessary for teachers to treat kids differently sometimes?

**Chapter 7:**

Did Joey hurt Maria on purpose? Do you think Joey is a good kid or a bad kid? Why?

**Chapter 8:**

Joey has to be sent to a special education school, away from his regular school. Do you think this is a good decision? Why or why not? Do you think that a special school can help Joey?

**Chapter 9:**

Maria's father thinks it's Joey's fault that he behaves the way he does. Do you agree with him? Why or why not? Do you think Joey's mom is a good mom to him? Why do you think that?

**Chapter 10:**

How does Joey feel about going to a new school? Have you ever had to start at a new school? What was it like? If you haven't, what do you think it would be like?

Most kids with all kinds of disabilities go to regular school instead of a special school the way they did a long time ago. Do you think this is better? Why or why not?

**Chapter 11:**

Joey tells his mother that he told Mr. Vanness and the diet lady about what his home life was like. Do you think he was right to talk about and share that? Why or why not? Why did Joey's mom seem like she wasn't happy about it? Do you think Joey's mom is trying to do a good job with him? How do you know?

Ed says the doctor's job is to get Joey the right medication and that Ed's job is to help Joey with his behavior so he can make the right decisions. How do you think Ed can help Joey control his behavior? What ways can you think of to be a help to kids who have trouble controlling their behavior sometimes?

**Chapter 12:**

What was Joey's relationship with his father like? What hurt him about it? Do you think not having his father around added to Joey's behavior problems?

What do you think about the way Joey's grandma treated him when he lived with her before his mother came to get him? Do you think it was abusive or mean? How do you think that might affect Joey's behavior?

**Chapter 13:**

Do you think Joey's mom should help him try to find his dad? Why or why not?

**Chapter 14:**

There are lots different kinds of medicine doctors give kids who have ADD. Sometimes they try different things until they find what works best. What kinds of medicine is the doctor going to have Joey try? How does it work? How is it different from the other medicine he was taking?

**Chapter 15:**

When Joey goes back to his regular school, the mother of one of the other students says to him, "… the medication has helped settle you down, but you have been a good kid all along. You are naturally good. I hope you know that about yourself. You have a good heart." What does she mean when she says that Joey is "naturally good"? Do you agree with her? Do you think the kids in your class who have behavior challenges know that they are good kids? How can you let them know that?

## *Jackson Whole Wyoming* by Joan Clark
## Book Club Discussion Questions for Students
## Topic: Asperger Syndrome

### Chapter 1:

Are there kids in your class like Jackson who don't have any friends?

What is the difference between kids you are nice to at school and friends you do things with outside of school? Tyler says Marcus makes fun of him and other students. Do you know someone like that?

Marcus says special ed. is for dumb kids. Do you agree with him? What do you know about special ed.?

### Chapter 2:

Jackson had to have his crayons lined up in a certain way. Sometimes kids with Asperger Syndrome (AS) have to do things in a special way that may seem strange to most people. Do you know someone with AS who has an odd habit? What is it? Do you think they can help it?

### Chapter 3:

Why do you think Tyler wished someone besides Jackson was his speech buddy? Have you ever been in a situation like that? What would be the best way to handle it? Kids with AS sometimes have a hard time when schedules change. Jackson started arguing with the teacher when he couldn't decorate his Easter bunny at 1:00 as he was told at first. Do you know a boy or girl with AS who has trouble when schedules change? What do they do? Why does Tyler think he has to back out of being the gift giver? Do you agree with him?

### Chapter 4:

Kids with AS have a hard time interacting with people and lots of times want to work with objects rather than be with people. What object is Tyler's cousin, Drew, and Jackson fascinated with?

Why do you think Jackson couldn't focus on his lesson until the fan was set a certain way? Do you think it was right of Marcus to tell on Jackson?

**Chapter 5:**

Do you think it was rude when Jackson kept pointing out that the guest to their class, Mr. Fletcher, didn't use monkey tails? Do you think Jackson could help it? Some kids with AS have a hard time understanding expressions, or sayings that other people can understand more or less automatically. One example would be when someone asks, "What's up?" This doesn't mean "what's on the ceiling?" or "what's up in the sky?" It means, "what's going on?" In the book, what did Mrs. Howard mean for Jackson to do when she told him to straighten up? What did Jackson do when she said that? Did he know what she really meant? Sometimes kids with AS don't understand jokes or things that other people think are funny, but they laugh anyway to try to fit in and be like everyone else. When Jackson stood up like a tin soldier and the other kids started laughing, Jackson laughed with them, and laughed really hard. Do you think he understood what was so funny to the other kids? If he didn't, why do you think he laughed?

**Chapter 6:**

Kids with AS often learn a lot about one or two things and like to talk about that all the time. Jackson's "area of special interest" is monkeys. He likes to read about them and talks about them a lot. Do you know someone with AS who has an area of special interest they know a lot about and like to talk about? Do you like to hear them talk about it? Do you think they talk about it too much? When they want to talk about their area of special interest, what can you do without being rude so you don't have to listen to it for a long time?

**Chapter 7:**

Tyler tells his mom he doesn't want to be the one to present the book to Jackson because Jackson is so weird and everyone will think he's weird too if he seems like he's Jackson's friend. Are you worried to be a friend to someone who is different or weird because then everyone will think you're different or weird, too? Tyler's mom says it's O.K. to be different. Do you agree or disagree? Tyler whispered to Jackson that Mrs. Smithers was being mean when she told him to keep himself in control. Jackson then repeated what Tyler said in a loud voice, "She was just being mean." He didn't know not to call a teacher mean out loud so everyone could hear. This is an example of a social skill a student with

AS might not have – knowing when to say something out loud and when not to. Do you know of a time when someone did something like this?

**Chapter 8:**

When his teacher said to get "all his things together" to take home, Jackson thought that he had to clear out everything he had in school. Often kids with AS go to the speech teacher to learn what expressions like this really mean. Do you know students who go to speech class? Do you know what they work on there?

**Chapter 9:**

Miss Wilson and Tyler's mom thought it was important that he understand what Asperger Syndrome is. Do you think it's important for kids to know what it is? Why or why not? At the end of the chapter Tyler says he hadn't shown good character. What does he mean by that? What does it mean to show good character? Can you think of a time you or someone else showed good character? Can you think of a time when you or someone else didn't show good character? Why is this important?

**Chapter 10:**

Tyler's mom says you should look at all the good in a person instead of trying to figure out the name of his problem. Do you agree or disagree? Miss Wilson says that kids like Drew and Jackson have trouble making friends and understanding people. Do you know kids like this? Do you think they can help it? Kids with AS act in certain ways because they have AS. What are some of the ways they have of acting, according to Miss Wilson and Tyler's mom? How do they behave that makes it hard for them to make friends?

**Chapter 11:**

Miss Berg described Jackson as a "trendsetter." What is a trendsetter? How did Marcus try to be mean to Jackson, and how did Tyler turn it around? Is there a way you could try to turn things around when one kid is being mean to another?

**Chapter 12:**

Jackson told Tyler that his mom and dad said he couldn't tell anyone he had Asperger Syndrome? Why do you think that is? What did it mean when Tyler said Jackson was "… just a kid with a problem, like the rest of us." Do you see kids who are different in that same way? Sometimes kids with AS can't tell the difference between when someone is being mean to them and when they are being nice to them. This can be seen when Jackson tells Tyler that Marcus is his friend. Do you know someone who has trouble telling when someone is their friend and when they are being mean to them? Is there anything you could do to help them when that happens? Tyler says that his cousin Drew doesn't have many friends and seems to like to play with things rather than kids. Do you think kids with AS want to have friends even though they have trouble knowing how to make them?

**Chapter 13:**

Jackson said in front of everyone, including Mr. Carson, that Mr. Carson's eyes looked weird. Kids with AS sometimes tell everything exactly the way it is, and talk about physical appearances (or how people look) even though it's considered rude. Have you ever known someone who did this? Can you think of something you could do to help them know not to do this?

Sometimes kids with AS have unique sensitivities, like Jackson who always wanted to touch people. Besides touching, they might try to smell or taste things more than other people do. Sometimes their hearing is especially sensitive and loud noises hurt their ears or upset them. How did Miss Berg get Jackson to stop touching other people?

**Chapter 14:**

Jackson had wanted the pinwheel all to himself and didn't want to share it with the other kids. He couldn't understand that they were just as interested in it as he was. Kids with AS sometimes have a hard time understanding the feelings of others. Can you think of a time when someone you know put themselves first and couldn't think of the other person? What could you do about that situation? Do you think it was right for Marcus to tell on Jackson that he was being rude? Do you think Jackson was rude on purpose? Did Jackson really tell a lie, and was he stealing the pinwheel?

**Chapter 15:**

Jackson is honest, even when it gets him in trouble. Do you know anyone else like that? Tyler's mom thinks that he shouldn't have asked Jackson about his having Asperger Syndrome. Do you agree with her? Do you think people should know if someone has AS? Why or why not? Tyler thinks he doesn't deserve to give Jackson the going-away present because he hasn't been a good enough friend to him. Do you agree with that? Why or why not?

**Chapter 16:**

Jackson had a hard time understanding why Tyler could "break" the rule and go into the classroom before the bell rang. Some kids with AS always want to make sure the rules are followed and have a hard time understanding when rules don't have to be followed perfectly each and every time. Have you ever known that to happen?

**Chapter 17:**

Tyler seems to understand Jackson better now and went out of his way when Jackson had his accident. Have you ever been able to help a friend or classmate when they were in trouble or made mistakes? Is this something you think kids ought to do?

**Chapter 18:**

Tyler tells his mom he hasn't been a real friend to Jackson. Do you think he has or hasn't? Do you think Jackson notices or minds? Do you think Jackson thinks Tyler is his friend? Should Tyler be the one to give Jackson the book?

**Chapter 19:**

Tyler says he's mad at himself for not sticking up for Jackson in the past and being a better friend to him. Have you ever felt like you weren't acting like a good enough friend to someone just because he or she was different? When a group of kids stuck together to laugh at Jackson's jokes and tell him he was funny, Marcus the bully finally stopped his teasing. Do you think this is a good way to get bullies to stop making fun of other kids?

**Chapter 20:**

Tyler told Mrs. Linn he looks at things differently because of Jackson. What do you think he meant by that?

**Chapter 21:**

At the end of the book is a poem Tyler wrote about Jackson. What have you learned about Asperger Syndrome from reading this book?

# RELATIONSHIP CIRCLES

Many children with social skills challenges have difficulty understanding social rules and setting boundaries. They struggle with knowing who to be close to and what kind of intimacy is appropriate. Take, for instance, the emotions of an 8th grader as illustrated in this poem written for a classroom assignment and read in front of the entire class before the teacher caught it. This girl was a mere acquaintance of the author. While a grownup may enjoy outpourings like this from a spouse (!), 8th-grade girls think this is weird and are embarrassed to be the object of this kind of affection.

Use Relationship Circles to help students choose appropriate behaviors in relating to the people in their lives, which in this instance means teaching a student that a poem like this one is reserved for people in his inner circles, not in his outer/acquaintance circles.

---

### *Ode to Samantha Price*

*I know a girl so pretty and nice,*
*And this person's name is Samantha Price.*
*You're more important to me than the bright golden sun,*
*Oh, when I am with you girl, my heart is having fun.*
*You're more important to me than the air that I breathe,*
*I know it's hard to say this and it's hard to believe,*
*But I love you. I need you, Samantha Price.*
*You and me, friends to the end,*
*Let's you and me start a brand new trend.*
*You make me feel feelings I've never felt,*
*And I love your sweet smile, it makes my heart melt.*
*I love you, I love you, girl,*
*I'd hit my knee just to have you.*
*I love you, I love you.*
*Kiss me and hug me.*
*I love you.*

*Signed,*
*A Broken-Hearted Boy,*
*Matt Morelli*

---

## Types of Relationship Circles[2]

Inner Circle:  You!

Next Circle:  Family members – People you can hug and share your deepest thoughts and feelings with.

Next Circle:  Your closest friends – People you eat lunch with, spend time at their house, or talk to most every day. No physical contact, but you can share some thoughts and feelings with people in this circle. Your friends are in this circle.

Outer Circle:  Acquaintances – People you say "hi" to in the halls at school or in your neighborhood. You don't share thoughts or feelings with them.

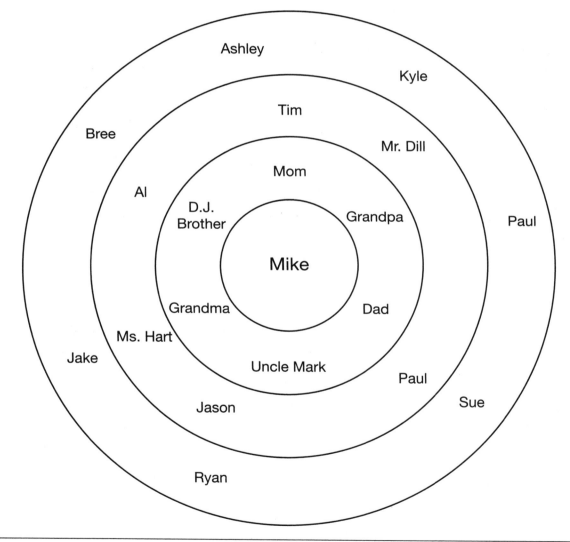

[2]Attwood, T. (1998). *Asperger Syndrome: A Guide for Parents and Professionals.* New York: Jessica Kingsley Publishers.

# Types of Relationship Circles

Inner Circle:  You!

Next Circle:  Family members – People you can hug and share your deepest thoughts and feelings with.

Next Circle:  Your closest friends – People you eat lunch with, spend time at their house, or talk to most every day. No physical contact, but you can share some thoughts and feelings with people in this circle. Your friends are in this circle.

Outer Circle:  Acquaintances – People you say "hi" to in the halls at school or in your neighborhood. You don't share thoughts or feelings with them.

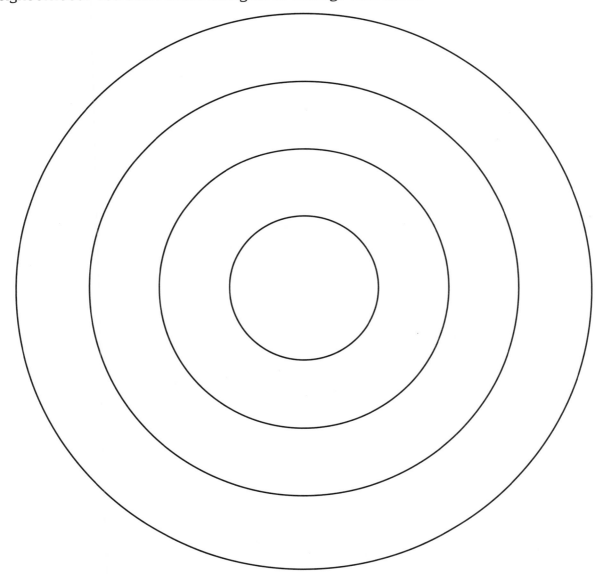

**Close Family**

**Close Friends**

**Acquaintances**

Look at the people in the illustrations above and discuss what they are doing. What makes them close family, close friends, or acquaintances? What are the differences between them?

# USING EXTRACURRICULAR ACTIVITIES TO PROMOTE FEELINGS OF BELONGING

As students with social skills challenges get older, particularly when they enter high school, often natural social connections just don't take place. The nuances of knowing when teenagers are being friendly, gossip, and dealing with understanding the complex world of the opposite sex can be all but indecipherable, and it's easy to get shut out. It doesn't take long for these kids to feel lonely as they listen to peers on Monday morning discuss the weekend activities they had no part in.

Since parents can no longer orchestrate play dates and birthday parties like they could when their child was younger, participation in extracurricular activities provides an important means of keeping these kids involved, busy, and feeling like they belong. It also helps provide social learning situations outside of the regular school day, and often can utilize a student's strengths and areas of special interest if a good match is made. But a student with social challenges cannot just be "thrown" into an extracurricular activity without ongoing teaching, feedback, and support. Read below for suggestions on providing a win-win situation for all involved.

# Example #1: Justin

## 1. Match student up with an activity he is interested in.

- Justin has Asperger Syndrome, has always been interested in sports statistics, and has a good memory for numbers. He is manager for the basketball team.

## 2. Match student with an adult who understands his needs and is willing to work with him.

- Mr. Smith, the school guidance counselor, works with kids with special needs as part of his job. He is also coach of the boys' basketball team.

## 3. Provide necessary support for the adult in charge of the extracurricular activity.

- Ms. Jones is one of the girls' high school basketball coaches and also works in the special education department. Since she is at most of the boys' basketball games anyway, she agrees to observe and provide feedback to Justin. This frees up the busy boys' basketball coach to not have to worry about Justin.

- Mrs. Baker, resource teacher, put on a workshop for the basketball team informing them of what Asperger Syndrome is and the behaviors they can expect to see out of Justin, with suggestions on how to respond.

## 4. Coach the student on appropriate behaviors and expectations.

- Mrs. Baker meets with the basketball coach to get a list of jobs Justin will have to do. She puts together an easy-to-read chart, puts it on a clipboard for Justin to use, and instructs him how to do each job and when each needs to be done.

- Justin's target behaviors are to follow adult instructions and give compliments when someone is doing something right instead of yelling insults when someone makes a mistake. Mrs. Baker writes Social Stories™ (http://www.thegraycenter.org) contrasting the appropriate and inappropriate ways for Justin to respond to the team when they do well and when they do poorly. She reads the Social Stories with Justin daily.

## 5. Use the child's Circle of Friends.

- Two basketball players, Jorden and Brady, have been chosen to be in Justin's Circle of Friends. They have been developing a relationship with Justin all year long and are there to encourage him as he manages the team.

- Jorden and Brady provided feedback to Mrs. Baker one day when Justin got upset because a spectator walked too close to the water cooler, resulting in him speaking inappropriately to her. Based on this feedback Mrs. Baker worked with Justin to teach appropriate behavior.

- Sometimes Justin gets so excited before a game starts, that he begins running crazily around the gym in circles, yelling to the team. When he starts to do this, Brady redirects him to his clipboard so Justin can once again focus on the tasks at hand.

## 6. Provide ongoing feedback.

- Every morning after a game, Mrs. Baker reviews the previous event, discussing what went well for Justin and addresses areas that require further work. Although this can be labor intensive at first, after a while and with proper training, Justin has become an indispensable member of the team and requires very little instruction, training, and monitoring. By his senior year, he is not only managing the basketball team, but the cross country and track teams as well, and is truly missed when he graduates.

# Example #2: Megan

## 1. Match student up with an activity she is interested in.

- Megan is a high school freshman with severe obsessive compulsive disorder and Tourette's Syndrome. One area of special interest to her is anything to do with movies. She has been hooked up with the theatre/drama department to work backstage in an upcoming play.

## 2. Match student with an adult who understands her needs and is willing to work with her.

- Mrs. Drake, the drama teacher, has experience with another student with obsessive compulsive disorder who is doing very well in the theatre department. Mrs. Drake has an easygoing personality that "goes with the flow." She has been told about Megan and is happy to include her in this group.

## 3. Provide support for the adult in charge of the extracurricular activity.

- One of Megan's main problems right now is targeting certain kids she wants to be friends with and then talking incessantly to them, sometimes even repeatedly text messaging and calling them at home when it's not welcome. Mrs. Baker, a resource teacher, is working with Megan and her family to teach social boundaries, appropriate conversation skills, and how to tell the difference between close friends and acquaintances.

## 4. Coach the student on appropriate behaviors and expectations.

- Megan is given a list of daily completion goals (see page 77) for theatre work. She meets with her resource teacher weekly (who has previously met with Megan's theatre teacher) and receives feedback.

## 5. Use the child's Circle of Friends.

- Megan has had a Circle of Friends in place for two years in middle school, but now that she is entering high school and joining a specialized group (theatre), three new students have been added. These girls are upper-class theatre students who already have their "place" in the group. They have been chosen because they are in theatre and also because they are confident and accepting of Megan's tics and obsessive behavior. One of the girl's has OCD herself that's under control now. She is very understanding of Megan's challenges.

## 6. Provide ongoing feedback.

- Mrs. Baker continues to challenge and instruct Megan with role-playing whenever she starts annoying kids with too much conversation and contact.

# Example #3: Andrew

## 1. Match student up with activity he is interested in.

- Andrew is a non-athletic, straight-A student who has difficulty interacting with others. He has chosen to participate in the school's Quiz Bowl and ACADEC (programs/clubs, where kids compete in academic subjects).

## 2. Match student with an adult who understands his needs and is willing to work with him.

- Mr. Hartman has run this program for years and is used to working with high-ability learners who struggle socially.

## 3. Provide support for adult in charge of the extracurricular activity.

- Mr. Hartman notices that during Quiz Bowl practice some students are calling Andrew names and snickering at him. Even though he has repeatedly told the kids to quiet down, they continue. Mrs. Baker, resource teacher, pulls the kids out one at a time during lunch to read the school handbook as it relates to harassment and bullying behavior. They are informed that the next step is an office referral. She continues to keep in touch with Mr. Hartman to get updates and intervene when necessary.

## 4. Coach the student on appropriate behaviors and expectations.

- Andrew is informed during resource time that his nose picking is grossing out the other students, resulting in them picking on him. He is given a squeeze ball to keep his hands busy during Quiz Bowl and ACADEC time.

## 5. Use the child's Circle of Friends.

- Matt, a student in Andrew's Circle of Friends, is also in Quiz Bowl and ACADEC. He quietly reminds Andrew to use his squeeze ball when he forgets and gives feedback to Mrs. Baker, the resource teacher.

## 6. Provide ongoing feedback.

- Mrs. Baker continues to touch base with Andrew, Matt, and Mr. Hartman to monitor the social situation.

# MEGAN'S WEEKLY THEATRE COMPLETION CHART

| | Mon. | Tues. | Wed. | Thurs. | Fri. |
|---|---|---|---|---|---|
| Handed out scripts | | | | | |
| Organized costumes | | | | | |
| Moved objects on set | | | | | |
| Listened to kids practice parts | | | | | |
| Helped with lights | | | | | |
| Worked on set artwork | | | | | |
| Had chats with other kids | | | | | |
| Put scripts away | | | | | |
| Helped clean auditorium | | | | | |

## DAILY COMPLETION CHART

| Task | Mon. | Tues. | Wed. | Thurs. | Fri. |
|------|------|-------|------|--------|------|
|      |      |       |      |        |      |
|      |      |       |      |        |      |
|      |      |       |      |        |      |
|      |      |       |      |        |      |
|      |      |       |      |        |      |
|      |      |       |      |        |      |
|      |      |       |      |        |      |
|      |      |       |      |        |      |
|      |      |       |      |        |      |

# "I Don't Want to" and "You Can't Make Me!"

Sometimes kids are resistant to trying new things, like participating in an activity they've never done before, even when it's in their best interest to do so. Discover how to handle a situation like this from the following vignette.

Tim is a junior in high school who has never been involved in any extracurricular activities, or much social life outside his home in general. His life consists of attending school, going home immediately afterwards, watching TV, and playing video games. He was raised in an abusive, neglectful home for the first six years of his life before his father was awarded custody of him. Tim has had some mental health issues in addition to academic struggles. He has come a long way since 8th grade in taking responsibility for his school work and following teacher instructions, but he does not talk or interact with peers and refuses his resource teacher, Mr. Harding's, encouragement to talk to other students, attend a football or basketball game, or join a club. Finally, Mr. Harding told Tim he had to join a club. As was typical for him, Tim told him he would absolutely not join a club and that Mr. Harding, "couldn't make him." Mr. Harding told Tim he would be discussing the matter with his parents in order to get their support in making Tim at least try it. Needless to say, Tim wasn't happy!

Tim's parents and his counselor came up with the agreement that he could get his learner's permit if he participated in Skills/VICA (a vocational skills club Mr. Harding recommended for Tim due to his interest and relative success in the school's woods, welding, and construction classes) for the school year. Since he was motivated to get his driver's license, Tim agreed. He reluctantly attended the first meeting, grumbling and arguing that he didn't want any part of it.

Mr. Harding communicated with Tim's parents about the first activity, which was a fundraising car wash. It was arranged that Tim would participate for two of the six hours. Tim was very nervous, so Mr. Harding spoke with the club leader ahead of time to find out exactly what Tim's jobs at the car wash would be, and then communicated those with Tim.

After the car wash, Tim's confidence began to grow, and he spent much of his free time pouring over the Skills/VICA activity calendar, becoming an enthusiastic member of the group, talking with other kids, and even attending conferences and competitions.

Just two months after joining a club, Tim felt confident enough to apply for not one, but two, part-time jobs outside of school, make it though the interviews, and land both jobs. If Tim had not been "forced" to participate in an extracurricular activity, it is probable that his life would still consist of only mandatory school attendance and television. The point is that at first many students are scared to death of participating in something new and different and will tell you so in no uncertain terms. Don't let them off the hook just because they are resistant at first. Work with the parents and the students to find a way to get them to at least try a new activity and give them the support they need to be successful in it. Don't be discouraged by their initial lack of enthusiasm for the idea.

## "We Aren't in Kansas Any More …"

Inevitably, extracurricular activities can end up with your students attending an event at a different school or facility. Fear of an unknown environment can lead to anxiety-driven behaviors, but these can be avoided if anticipated and addressed ahead of time. Although it may seem labor intensive at first, very quickly you'll find your students becoming independent and confident of what is expected of them. Some suggestions for a smooth, successful experience include the following.

- Talk to the event sponsor ahead of time to learn as much as possible about the upcoming day's events. Then share these details with your student.

- Share schedules ahead of time with your students and their parents. (Often students forget to tell their parents.)

- If your school has a printed daily bulletin, get a copy for your student. Also, give her a copy of the school calendar so she will have a visual of upcoming events ahead of time.

- Pair your student up with a buddy (preferably someone from her Circle of Friends) who can help out if needed. Make sure the child knows who this buddy will be.

- Let the bus driver know who your student is, that she may be anxious the first time out, and ask him to keep an extra eye on her.

- If your student is anxious and enjoys music, you might talk to her parents about her bringing a CD player or iPod to listen to on the bus. This is what many of the other students will be doing, too.

- Look at a map ahead of time showing where they'll be going for the event. You may also be able to find a map of the facility on its website.

- If the student is a team manager, give her a clipboard and a list of duties she will be expected to perform. Acquaint her with several students she can ask questions so she won't have to go to the coach/sponsor each time.

- Some students may need a place that feels safe if they become anxious or overstimulated away from home. Discuss with the sponsor the importance of designating a room/hallway when first arriving where the student knows she can go if she has to temporarily remove herself from a stressful situation.

- Use the Extracurricular Activities Checklist on the following page to cover all bases before, during, and after the event. Place a mark in square in each row after task has been completed. The chart has enough spaces for 14 different events.

- Meet with kids from her Circle of Friends ahead of time to strategize ways to help the student experience success at the event.

- Troubleshoot after the event with both the event sponsor or coach and peers to plan how to make the next event even more successful for the student.

# EXTRACURRICULAR ACTIVITIES CHECKLIST

| **BEFORE EVENT:** | | | | | | | | | | | | | | | |
|---|---|---|---|---|---|---|---|---|---|---|---|---|---|---|---|
| Notified student of club/event/expectations | | | | | | | | | | | | | | | |
| Talked to parents regarding participation | | | | | | | | | | | | | | | |
| Met with event sponsor to discuss needs/expectations | | | | | | | | | | | | | | | |
| Met with Circle of Friends kids about student/event | | | | | | | | | | | | | | | |
| Got list of duties for student | | | | | | | | | | | | | | | |
| Directed student to bulletin/announcements to learn more | | | | | | | | | | | | | | | |
| **IF EVENT IS AWAY:** | | | | | | | | | | | | | | | |
| Spoke with bus driver | | | | | | | | | | | | | | | |
| Informed parents of details | | | | | | | | | | | | | | | |
| Discussed travel behavior | | | | | | | | | | | | | | | |
| Looked at map showing where event is taking place | | | | | | | | | | | | | | | |
| Talked to sponsor about "home away from home" base | | | | | | | | | | | | | | | |
| **AFTER EVENT:** | | | | | | | | | | | | | | | |
| Talked with student | | | | | | | | | | | | | | | |
| Talked with sponsor | | | | | | | | | | | | | | | |
| Talked with Circle of Friends kids | | | | | | | | | | | | | | | |

# Extracurricular Activities – Sample Possibilities

- Theatre (can act or work behind the scenes)

- Speech

- Skills/VICA (Vocational Industrial Clubs of America)

- One-act plays

- Debate team

- Sports, including intramurals

- Sports team managers or assistant managers

- Concession stand workers

- Assistant to athletic director

- FFA (National FFA Organization – Agricultural Science Education)

- Foreign Language Club

- Photography Club

- Chess Club

- Art Club

- Pokémon Club

- Anime Club

- Choir/singing/band groups

- Flag Corp

- Volunteering at church or charitable organization

# REAL-LIFE CIRCLE SUCCESSES

The following situations illustrate what a Circle of Friends can do.

- Andrew has Asperger Syndrome, and the kids on his school bus have been teaching him to call other kids vulgar names. Andrew has no idea what the words mean, but likes the attention he's getting from his peers. Hannah, a girl from his Circle told the teasers to stop it, but they wouldn't. She made Andrew's Circle facilitator aware of the situation. The kids who were teasing were then dealt with by the adults at the school. Also, both Andrew's parents and his resource teacher were made aware of the situation so they could teach him how to identify when he was being made fun of and strategies to use to deal with the problem.

- Juanita, diagnosed with obsessive compulsive disorder, recently cut her hair until it was only a couple of inches long. Although her parents took her to a hair stylist to try to remedy the situation, it was still obvious that something wasn't quite right with the cut. Juanita was so self-conscious of her looks and disappointed in herself for what she had done that she was having a difficult time coming to school. Her mother called her Circle facilitator to explain the situation, and a Circle meeting was called first thing the next morning. The Circle kids were told what had happened and instructed to try to make Juanita feel especially welcome at school that day. They met her at the school entrance and took over from there, making what could have been a very difficult day a bit easier for Juanita.

- Daniel is a 13-year-old who has lived in foster homes and residential treatment facilities since he was 6. This is the 10th school he has attended, and he's trying to fit in and get attention. Daniel came to school with a habit of putting people down by calling them names and threatening with gang-related signs. Daniel's Circle was instructed to give him daily attention by having at least 1-2 conversations with him, and inviting him to eat lunch at their tables every few days or so. His Circle was also instructed to either ignore Daniel's name calling or tell him that it hurts their feelings and that they don't like it when he calls them names and does mean things. After two weeks of these positive interactions, Daniel's office referrals decreased by 90%.

- Josh, a freshman with Asperger Syndrome, can get overstimulated during lunch with all the noise and commotion that accompany this time of day. One day after eating, he grabbed an empty cart in the hallway and started pushing it crazily as fast as he could. Hilary, one of his Circle friends, saw what was happening, caught up with Josh, took the cart away from him, and engaged him in a conversation to calm him down.

- Kyle, a sophomore with ASD, was obsessed with piercing his ears. Unknown to his parents and teachers, one day he took a needle from home and in choir class, stuck it through his ear lobe, immediately becoming very upset with what he had done. He knelt on the floor and began to cry. Unfortunately, there was a substitute teacher in class that day who had no idea what was happening. One of Kyle's Circle friends explained to the sub that Kyle had special needs and had to find his resource teacher right away. He walked with Kyle to find the help he needed.

- Saya is a 15-year-old English Language Learner whose family escaped from Iraq under traumatic circumstances. Once in the United States, her parents attempted to set up a marriage between Saya and a 40-year-old man, also from their homeland. After Saya expressed her refusal to go along with her parents' wishes and communicated this to a teacher at school, Social Services was called and Saya was temporarily sent to a foster home and a new school until the situation could be straightened out. Not only was Saya experiencing trauma resulting from leaving her home country and dealing with a new culture where she cannot understand the language, she was also in an unfamiliar home and school. It was discovered one day that she was not eating lunch. She was terrified to go into the lunchroom and instead hid in the girls' locker room. Saya, who had shown an interest in playing basketball, was put on an intramural team, and a Circle of Friends was made up of girls on her team. Saya started eating in the cafeteria with her Circle friends and began learning English quickly once she had more contact with her peers throughout the day.

- Ian is a high school student with ASD. Although he is a straight-A student, he became depressed towards the end of his sophomore year, expressing feelings of isolation and boredom with nothing to do after the school day ended. A voracious sports fan with an interest in sports statistics, Ian was made manager of the cross-country, basketball, and track teams. This not only occupied his time and used his talents to help others, it also gave him the opportunity to practice his social skills. Having seen students of the opposite sex hug each other, Ian started to hug girls during track practice, sometimes pulling them to the ground and lying on top of them. Needless to say, the girls were beginning to feel uncomfortable with Ian's inappropriate behavior. One of Ian's Circle friends told his Circle facilitator about his behavior on the track field. The facilitator was then able to work with Ian on the concept of staying out of others' personal space, as well as appropriate and inappropriate touching.

- Sarah is a 6th-grade girl living in a group home in the district. Her placement resulted from her having been a victim of sexual abuse and the discovery that she had been exposed to pornography repeatedly from the time she was a young child. Two of her Circle friends approached the Circle facilitator to communicate the fact that Sarah was discussing inappropriate topics of a sexual nature that were making her peers uncomfortable. Armed with that information, her Circle facilitator can work with her on more appropriate topics of conversation.

- Simone has to do a project for her 9th-grade science class where she has to write a survey and give it to 10 other students to obtain the required data. Simone, who is an English Language Learner, is anxious about doing this because she is embarrassed by her poor English and having to talk to people she doesn't know. Her teacher recommended she ask her Circle friends to take the survey, and Simone was much more comfortable approaching kids who knew her and her situation.

# WITH OPEN ARMS – OPENING EVEN WIDER BY ENGAGING TEACHERS IN LEARNING TEAMS

Once a peer support group is established, it is important to take social immersion a step further by teaching the school personnel the target child comes into contact with on a daily basis how to best interact with him. All too often, it is left to special educators and other support staff to take full responsibility for the child with social challenges, depriving him of even more social opportunities. A broader approach like the one introduced here makes sense when we consider the inclusion models used in schools today.

## Imagine This – Scenario One:

Mrs. Smith is an 8th-grade English teacher responsible for nearly 140 hormone-driven students daily. She has to see that they improve their writing in readiness for high school, do well enough on state standards to satisfy administrators and the public who will read the test scores in the local newspaper, make daily lessons interesting, engaging, and worthwhile, and, did we mention make sure everyone gets along and treats each other nicely? These students can run the gamut from being high-ability learners to having mental retardation. In addition, there is lunch detention, hall monitoring, team meetings, student-led conferences, and continuing education credits that must be continually earned.

Let's imagine Mrs. Smith has one student in nearly every class who has social challenges, whether due to a disability like autism or ADD, a distressing group home or foster care placement, or being an English Language Learner unfamiliar with American culture. These children may quietly drown in isolation or experience full-blown meltdowns when Mrs. Smith merely changes the schedule. They can cause disruptions in the classroom, pick their noses, obsess on a member of the opposite sex, or constantly show off to get attention from their peers. These kids can get on an already overworked, stressed-out teacher like Mrs. Smith's last nerve.

## Scenario Two:

Mr. George, the high school principal, sits staring across his desk at Shawn trying to re-member just how many times this student has had an office referral this school year. He is not sure, because they are too numerous to count. Shawn's most recent offense involved making sexually inappropriate comments to a female student. He has regularly been in fights with his peers and disrespects teachers in his attempts to gain acceptance at this new school, his seventh in as many years. He has had lectures, detentions, and suspen-sions. Nothing seems to have significantly changed his behavior. Mr. George knows an-other five-day out-of-school suspension won't make much of a difference, but Mr. George, not to mention Shawn's teachers, would sure appreciate the respite from him.

Teachers and administrators aren't the only ones who interact with your socially chal-lenged students in the school setting. Don't forget to include ALL personnel your target child may come in contact with in the school as you work towards your goal of creating a total community of support. Tech support, bus drivers, custodians, media specialists, and cafeteria workers are just a few of the support staff who could benefit from learning about the student and be encouraged to interact with her. These folks can play an important role in the life of the child.

## When the Computer Guys Get Cranky ...

Jason's Asperger Syndrome sometimes gets him into trouble at school. This highly intel-ligent sophomore is currently obsessing on sexual issues. His curiosity is normal for a 15-

year-old male, but his inability to shut it off during school hours is not. Jason has somehow managed to evade the Internet blocks put on the school computers, and for the third time this year has gotten onto a site containing inappropriate content. The first time this happens, school policy dictates the student loses all computer access for six weeks. However, the school computer network administrators grudgingly shortened computer restriction for Jason to two weeks after the first offense when the resource teacher attempted to explain his special needs to them. The second time it happened, Jason's resource teacher had to get the school psychologist involved so Jason would not be denied computer access for the remainder of the school year, the normal second-offense consequence.

Although Jason is receiving consequences, reviewing Social Stories™ (http://www. thegraycenter.org) daily, and has a plan to cope appropriately with his sexual urges, the special education staff knows it will take time before he fully integrates this concept and demonstrates appropriate behavior one hundred percent of the time. At this point there is a communication problem and disagreement regarding solutions between the computer guys who do not tolerate this behavior from any other student in the building and the resource teacher who knows that Jason needs access to the computer so he can practice appropriate Internet behavior, a skill that will be essential to his future success in the "real world" after high school. The network administrators have issued an ultimatum: Jason is off the computer for the remainder of the school year, no matter what!

Don't misunderstand. Teachers and administrators go into the teaching profession because they love kids and want to help them become productive, happy young adults. But without proper support and education, they can unintentionally do harm, either by ignoring or giving negative feedback to students with social challenges on a regular basis. Fortunately for Jason, when network administrators learned about AS, a workable plan was developed so he could continue to practice appropriate computer use.

By implementing a Circle of Friends with the students in your school, you help change behaviors through positive peer integration. But the social climate can be further optimized by supporting staff through implementation of Learning Teams. Read on to learn how to encourage Learning Teams in your school.

# Learning Team Basics

## *Commonly Asked Questions*

### What is a Learning Team?

A Learning Team (Roberts & Pruitt, 2003) is a small, collaborative group of school staff who work together in a structured way, creating professional learning communities as they focus on an issue that affects the school/classroom environment.

### Who is on the Learning Team?

Within this context, any adult who has contact with the target student may be on the Learning Team. This can include teachers, administrators, and support staff.

### What does a Learning Team do?

A Learning Team focuses on staff education to address specific student needs. A Learning Team designed to help staff work better with socially challenged students, for example, uses materials and discusses issues that will give teachers, administrators, and support staff tools to better work with specific kids.

### What are the advantages of a Learning Team?

It's economical, both in monetary cost and time. Learning Teams help develop empathy on the part of staff while at the same time giving them practical ideas to use with kids with social challenges.

### How does a Learning Team work?

The members of the Learning Team read a book that deals with issues our kids face and then come back as a group, usually for 30-45 minutes every week or every other week, to discuss the book and how it relates to particular students. A special emphasis is put on developing a plan to optimize the classroom environment so these kids can be successful and teachers aren't distracted from their teaching by their behaviors.

## How many people are on the Learning Team?

It is recommended to limit the number of participants to no more than 10 or so. If the group gets larger than that, you might find some members do not participate fully in the process.

## What is the cost?

Whatever it costs to get a set of books for the group to read. If the book chosen costs $12.95 and there are eight members of the Learning Team, the cost would be approximately $100. Once this initial investment is made, the books can be reused in the future.

## When does the Learning Team meet?

The Learning Team can meet before school, after school, during plan time, or when doing summer work.

## Who leads the Learning Team?

The person who knows the student best usually leads the Learning Team. It is often the student's case manager or a special education teacher, but may be a guidance counselor or administrator. Leaders may be rotated throughout the course of Learning Team meetings, with people taking turns to lead each week.

## What is the role of the Learning Team leader?

The role of the leader is to choose the book to be read, organize the meeting schedule, and facilitate discussion among group members. His role includes providing discussion questions, keeping the group on task, keeping the conversation positive and productive, and guiding groups in creating a proactive plan to successfully work with the students.

## How long does the Learning Team last?

It runs until the book is completed. A usual assignment is approximately 50 pages to be read ahead of time, or whenever you come to a good stopping place. For example, if the team chose a 200-page book, reading approximately 50 pages each time, meeting 30 minutes every other week, the total course of the topic would run eight weeks, with the team meeting four times.

**But, we don't have the time to do a Learning Team!!!!**

You don't have time to NOT do a Learning Team! Add up all the time a teacher, administrator, or bus driver spends on repeated social/behavioral issues. A Learning Team is a proactive way to decrease the problem behaviors and distractions that result from poor social skills in the school environment.

**What kinds of books are used in Learning Teams?**

Choose books that discuss social struggles similar to those of the child/children you're focusing on. For instance, if you have a child with Asperger Syndrome, choose a book that deals with that issue. An Internet search or conversation with your school librarian will most likely turn up more options than you could ever hope for. Possible titles are included in this book, along with discussion questions you can use. It is suggested you avoid "textbook-y" selections filled with difficult terminology, long, and otherwise difficult books for the layperson to wade through. Excellent results can be obtained with either fiction or books that include case studies staff can relate to. Humor never hurts either!

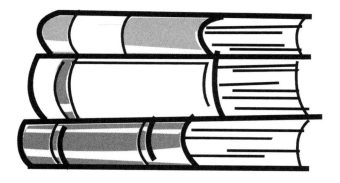

# Learning Team Book Study Guide Discussion Questions

- Choose a book that relates to the target student/s. Books that are enjoyable and easy to read are preferable.

- Develop a set of thought-provoking questions that will result in greater understanding of the child's struggles. You can often find discussion questions on a particular book with an Internet search. Don't worry if you don't get through each and every question; time constrictions may not allow it. The purpose of a Learning Team is to set the stage for learning, communication, and brainstorming how to apply new ideas to help kids you're all working with.

- Set a meeting and reading schedule and invite any adults who work with the student.

- Give participants discussion questions ahead of time to promote more focused discussion at your meetings.

- After discussing how the book relates to the challenges of the child and the people in his life, brainstorm and communicate a plan for how to effectively help him develop his social skills.

- Keep the discussion positive.

- Have fun at your team meetings. A sense of humor (along with some snacks) helps everyone have a worthwhile time.

## Possible Book Selections for Learning Team Use

*(Refer to the Book Club selections on pages 46-49 for additional recommendations.)*

## ADD

***Putting on the Brakes* by Patricia O. Quinn, M.D., and Judith M. Stern, M.A.**

This book is a great guide for young people, parents, and professionals, outlining what ADD is, how to know if you have it, brain function in people with ADD, and how to cope with this condition. This book is short, easy to read, and filled with practical tips on how to help students with ADD.

### *Adolescents and ADD* by Patricia O. Quinn, M.D.

This is another short guide book with medication information and case studies to help understand what life with ADD is like.

### *Driven to Distraction* by Edward Hallowell, M.D.

This interesting book explains ADD along the spectrum of life from childhood to adulthood. Case studies and effective coping strategies are presented by an expert who knows first-hand the effects of this condition as he and some family members have ADD themselves. Dr. Hallowell is also the author of *Answers to Distraction*, another fine selection.

### *Joey Pigza Swallowed the Key* and *Joey Pigza Loses Control* by Jack Gantos

Both of these juvenile fiction books written for folks ages 10 and up chronicle the difficulties of Joey, an 11-year-old with ADD. The books are told from Joey's perspective and let the reader walk in the shoes of a person living the chaotic life of untreated ADD and later on when the condition is under control. The series illustrates the changes that can occur when appropriate interventions are put in place. Teachers will recognize the challenges these students can bring to the classroom as Joey is similar to the students they encounter on a regular basis. These are good selections if you're trying to get past the "He could do the work if he wanted to … he's just lazy and making poor choices!" attitudes in your particular school.

## Asperger Syndrome

### *The Curious Incident of the Dog in the Night-Time* by Mark Haddon

This humorous, sometimes sad, always suspense-filled fictional book puts the reader in the mind of an adolescent with Asperger Syndrome as he tries to navigate his complex social world while trying to solve the mysterious death of a neighbor's dog. This is a bestselling book you won't be able to put down.

### *Jackson Whole Wyoming* by Joan Clark

This juvenile fiction book tells the story of the relationship between a neurotypical 5th grader and his fellow classmate with AS. It addresses the conflict between the desire to be kind to an unusual peer while trying to fit into the confusing world of middle school students. This book is touching and easy to read.

### *What Is Asperger Syndrome and How Will It Affect Me?* by Martine Ives

This is a guide written for young people, but perfect for staff who say they don't have time for a Learning Team. Twenty-seven pages cover to cover, this book explains AS in an easy-to-understand, no-nonsense way.

### *Freaks, Geeks, and Asperger Syndrome* by Luke Jackson

This delightful book is written by a teenager with AS. A few of the topics include characteristics of AS, how and when to tell people, school difficulties and possible solutions, bullying, ways to win friends and influence people, and dating. The book is highly recommended to help your staff understand what life is like for kids with AS.

### *A 5 Is Against the Law! Social Boundaries: Straight Up!* by Kari Dunn Buron

Written for adolescents and young adults, *A 5 Is Against the Law!* focuses on behaviors that can get kids who don't understand social boundaries in trouble with the law. This book is filled with examples and hands-on activities.

## General Behavioral Issues

### *The Explosive Child* by Ross Greene, Ph.D.

This book is a must-read for schools with chronically frustrated, non-compliant, "explosive" students. The case studies make the concepts easy to understand and help develop empathy for the difficult world these kids encounter daily. It goes beyond explanations, giving practical tips for working with hard to handle children using a workable Plan A, Plan B, and Plan C system.

### *There's a Boy in the Girls' Bathroom* by Louis Sachar

In this juvenile fiction book, the reader meets friendless Bradley Chalkers, who cannot relate to adults or peers and consistently fails his upper-elementary classes. Jeff, a new boy at school, wants to become friends with Bradley. While he is mean to him at some points in order to gain acceptance from others, he shows persistence in the end in befriending him and helping him change his ways. Topics addressed include bullying, poor social skills, making friends, and acceptance of individual differences.

# *The Explosive Child* by Ross W. Greene, Ph.D.
## Learning Team Discussion Questions (Inflexible/explosive kids)

Written for parents, educators, and professionals who live and work with hard-to-manage, easily frustrated children of all ages, this practical, easy-to-read book outlines how to understand these kids and move from using reinforcement systems that don't work to teaching communication and problem solving skills that do. A must-read book for anyone interacting with inflexible, explosive children.

## Chapter 1:

1. Having read this chapter, what have you learned about inflexible, explosive children you previously weren't aware of? How do you think it would feel to be the parent of a child with these difficulties?

## Chapter 2:

1. In this section, flexibility and tolerance of frustration are described as skills children need to learn, much like acquiring math, reading, and athletic skills. Some children do not progress in a normal developmental fashion in this area and in fact, are developmentally delayed. Do you accept this premise? Why or why not?

2. Describe some of the brain irregularities that could come into play in children who are inflexible, intolerant, and frustrated. Do you and your colleagues view inflexible/explosive behaviors as (A) "the result of a brain based failure to progress developmentally" or (B) "planned, intentional, and purposeful"? (p. 14)

3. Have you used strategies to "teach the child who's boss"? What were they? Were they effective? How did you feel afterwards?

4. How could the author's descriptions of "Common Characteristics of Inflexible-Explosive Children" be more helpful than the diagnostic criteria? (pp. 15-18)

5. Discuss the following phases of an inflexible-explosive episode: vapor lock, crossroads, and meltdown. Can you identify these phases in a previous interaction you have had with a child? What mistakes have you made in working with children in these phases?

**Chapter 3:**

1.  In Chapter 3, the author presents the following specific pathways that can result in a "chronic pattern of vapor lock and meltdowns":

    *   difficult temperaments
    *   ADHD and executive function deficits
    *   social skill deficits
    *   language processing
    *   mood and anxiety
    *   nonverbal learning disability
    *   sensory integration dysfunction

    Discuss several things you learned about each of these areas, and if possible, relate some of them to a child you're working with.

2.  List the three "files" (p. 34) needed for the executive skill of working memory. Discuss a situation one of your students with ADD struggles with due to possible impaired working memory.

3.  There is a description of the complexities involved in processing a social interaction on pp. 38-39. Discuss a social interaction your students struggled with recently. Can you recognize difficulties they encountered due to poor automatic processing?

4.  Describe an interaction you have experienced with a child who does not have the skills necessary to recognize the impact her behavior has on those around her.

5.  One important language processing skill some children lack is a large vocabulary of words to describe their emotions. Can you think of students you work with who use inappropriate expressions to convey feelings due to their poor repertoire of emotion-describing words?

6.  Discuss this statement: "We adults tend to take things far less personally and respond far more emphatically to children who cry when they're frustrated instead of explode, even though the two behaviors often flow from the same source" (p. 48). Is it possible for you as an educator to feel empathy rather than anger when a student has an inappropriate, explosive incident?

7. Describe the difference between viewing pathways as excuses rather than explanations. What is the danger in viewing them as excuses?

## Chapter 4:

1. What did Helen's parents want from Helen at dinner time? Did they get what they wanted? Do you think Helen will learn new behavior from this episode and apply it to the next similar situation? Why or why not?

2. What factors help explain Helen's inability to deal with her frustration? (pp. 65-66)

3. Discuss the statement: "I'm all in favor of punishment when it's productive … when it's effective in changing a child's behavior. But I'm not real keen on punishment just for the sake of punishment" (p. 73). Do you agree or disagree?

4. How could viewing Danny as "grumpy and irritable" instead of "disrespectful and oppositional" change the way adults interact with him? (p. 74)

5. Discuss the possibility of teachers serving as "surrogate frontal lobes" (p. 78) for students who need them. What does this mean?

6. On p. 84, Dr. Greene writes, "We're not going to get anywhere unless I can establish a relationship with him," referring to establishing a relationship with Mitchell. How do you attempt to establish positive relationships with your inflexible-explosive students?

## Chapter 5:

1. Discuss the standard behavior management approach outlined on pp. 87 and 88. Have you used behavior management approaches that haven't worked with certain students? With what you've previously read in this book, why might this approach not be effective in changing the behavior of inflexible-explosive children?

2. The author maintains that inflexible-explosive children already know what good behavior is expected of them and are motivated to behave appropriately. Do you agree?

3. Discuss the two criteria Amy lacked (pp. 93-94) to succeed with a behavior management program.

4. Discuss the statement: "If [a child] is going to learn to be more flexible … it's not going to happen by your being a role model for inflexibility." Could "showing who's boss" actually fuel meltdowns in inflexible-explosive children?

5. Discuss the statement: "Teaching a child 'who's boss' is easy; understanding and responding to a child's deficits in the areas of flexibility and frustration tolerance is a lot harder." Do you have students where the "showing who's boss" approach hasn't worked? Why do you think this is?

## Chapter 6:

1. Describe the creation of a "user-friendlier" environment for an inflexible-explosive child. List several specific things you could do personally to create a user-friendlier environment for your inflexible-explosive child.

2. What is meant by "reciprocal inflexibility"?

3. Discuss this statement, "Lifeguards who watch the water closely don't have to jump in and rescue people very often." It's important for adults to recognize early warning signs of vapor lock. How does your student communicate when frustration is beginning to set in?

4. The author maintains that demonstrating empathy is one way to avoid a meltdown. Reread the Mother-Addie interaction (pp. 112-114) and discuss how Mother dealt with her daughter's resistance. Apply this process to a situation you've had in the past with an inflexible-explosive child, by talking/thinking though how you could have handled things.

5. Another technique mentioned is distraction, possibly with humor. Can you think of a situation this could work in with one of your inflexible students?

6. Discuss the "downshifting" that Lydia's parents could have used in the car incident (pp. 115-117). Do you think the second response would enable rather than teach Lydia? Do you think Lydia's parents' response was effective in teaching her to change her behavior in the future?

7. Why isn't ignoring effective with these kids when they are in vapor lock stage?

8. What is another way to interpret "screw you" and other disrespectful remarks? (p. 118)

9. Describe an incident when you fueled a child's inflexibility-explosiveness.

10. Discuss terminology/vocabulary that might be more effective in communicating about or with a child you are trying to help in place of terms such as "bratty," "manipulative," "attention seeking," "stubborn," "controlling," and "angry" (p. 120). How can you as an educator actively teach this more effective vocabulary to your students?

11. Do you think Craig's father's carrying his firefighter equipment at the fair for him was enabling and harmful because Craig got his own way? Or do you think this was an action taken to create a user-friendlier environment? Discuss.

12. On p. 128 there is a summary of how to create a user-friendlier environment. Apply some or all eight components to a specific child you work with to create a user-friendlier environment in your classroom.

## Chapter 7:

1. What are the differences between Basket A, Basket B, and Basket C behaviors and what specific goals do each help a child reach? (p. 133) What types of behaviors would go in each basket?

2. Think of one of your inflexible-explosive students and list his problematic behaviors. Then label each behavior as either Basket A, Basket B, or Basket C behaviors.

3. What can you say to let a child know a behavior is in Basket A? (p. 135) Why are there few behaviors in Basket A? Make a list of possible Basket A behaviors in the school setting.

4. Why is Basket B the most important basket? (p. 136) What skills will a child learn when an adult works things out with him in Basket B?

5. Discuss how a child will know a behavior is in Basket B using the concepts of empathy and invitation. Practice a conversation you could have with a child identifying a Basket B behavior using empathy and invitation. Make a list of possible Basket B behaviors for a particular student.

6. Describe how ignoring Basket C behaviors actually helps the goal of safety. Make a list of possible Basket behaviors for a particular student of yours.

7. Describe the difference between "giving in" and intentionally placing a behavior in Basket C.

## IMPORTANT POINT!

The adult is still in charge as illustrated by the answers to the following questions:

Q: Who decides whether an acceptable solution has been reached?

A: You.

Q: Who decides what basket a behavior is in?

A: You.

Q: Who decides whether a child is actually capable of following through on a potential solution?

A: You.

Q: Who's still in charge?

A: You.*

(* from p. 152)

8. Discuss the concept of addressing a Basket B behavior "Outside the Moment." Choose a specific possible Basket B behavior and child, and then brainstorm how/ when to address it "outside the moment" in the school setting.

9. How would you respond to Helen's dad's comment, "The real world doesn't have baskets in it or people who always try to understand."

10. Discuss the ineffective patterns of basket use that could result in lack of success in changing behavior (pp. 164-177).

11. The author states that he is "not enthusiastic about putting the completion of homework into Basket A" (p. 168). What are your thoughts as an educator on this topic? Do you see cases where it might be beneficial to lessen or even eliminate homework in order to bring about behavior change in the long run?

12. How do you feel about not putting swearing in Basket A?

13. Some children are able to tolerate waiting while you decide which basket a particular behavior should be placed in. Do you have a feeling for which of your inflexible-explosive children can wait and which ones can't? Can you think of instances where delaying a discussion of a Basket B behavior might be beneficial?

## Chapter 8:

1. Under what circumstances could a child benefit from medication?

2. Is there a "collaborative spirit" between you, the educator, and your students' parents regarding medication status? Do you think this communication is important? Why or why not? How could this be facilitated?

## Chapter 9:

1. Can you relate to Andy's father's response to his communication when asked to turn the TV off? Have you ever communicated with a non-compliant student the way Andy's father did? What was the outcome? Brainstorm an alternative response.

2. What does swearing indicate? (p. 202) What response can be given when swearing occurs in the classroom in a way that helps you maintain an air of authority in front of the other students, letting them know that swearing is inappropriate, yet helps the student work through a Basket B behavior? Practice what you could say/do in that moment.

3. Besides swearing, what other words have you heard your inflexible-explosive students use in place of more sophisticated vocabulary.

4. Are there statements you can make as an educator to help change an erroneous perception of self in a child with an inflexible belief system? Practice saying them.

## Chapter 10:

1. Although this chapter deals with family matters as opposed to school matters, Dr. Greene presents several maladaptive communication patterns that adults in the school environments also use. What are some of these ineffective patterns? Do you

find yourself communicating with some of your students using them? If so, when and with whom?

2.  Practice saying or write down statements to use in place of the following problematic communication patterns:

| Poor Communication | Better Communication |
|---|---|
| A) Speculation | Use an "I" statement |
| B) Overgeneralization | Phrase things tentatively |
| C) Perfectionism | Put the situation in perspective |
| D) Sarcasm | Say what you really mean |
| E) Catastrophizing | Speak positively |
| F) Interrupting | Practice active listening |
| G) Lecturing | Practice short, concise communication |
| H) Dwelling on the past | Present-oriented statements |
| I) Talking though a third person | Speak for yourself |

## Chapter 11:

1.  Read the questions posed in this chapter, discussing your own possible responses to them and the actual responses given. Do you agree? Why or why not?

2.  Discuss having a child make amends rather than accepting a punishment. Are there situations in the classroom when making amends might be more effective than taking a punishment? What could that look like?

3.  Do you ever threaten your students with a consequence you cannot follow through with? Why is this harmful? Why does this happen and what could you do instead?

4.  In the discussion on use of timeouts, it is recommended that it can be productive to have parents and children "go their separate ways" when the atmosphere is in vapor lock approaching meltdown. Is this possible in the school setting when the same situation presents itself? What could this look like in your school? Can you come up with a plan to provide this temporary separation?

5.  Discuss the statement: "When in doubt, respond as if your child's behavior is unplanned and unintentional." Do you agree or disagree? (p. 248)

6. Discuss the views presented in this chapter of ADD and lying. Do you see evidence of this in some of your students? Do you agree or disagree that lying is the direct result of the inability of the child with ADD to quickly process information and demonstrate impulse control? Why or why not?

7. Discuss the author's assertion that the terms "manipulation" and "taking responsibility" are overused. Do you agree or disagree? Why?

8. Teachers often feel that with so many other responsibilities, they don't have time to implement strategies for a small number of (or even just one) inflexible-explosive child. Discuss the following three ideas presented on pp. 251-252 and brainstorm ways you could incorporate them in the classroom, and/or how you could access and use support personnel to assist you. Who can be designated/delegated to do what?

   • "Make adaptations" – establish priorities and remove frustrations

   • "Perform tasks for the child he's unable to do right now"

   • "Create a mechanism for a child to improve his/her awareness of time in general"

9. Has there ever been an instance where you were baffled by a student's frustration because the cause of it or the time frame within which it happened had nothing to do with you? How did you respond? Practice words you could use with a child if you found yourself in this situation.

10. "Clarity is your friend and ambiguity your enemy" (p. 255). Discuss. Practice using statements of clarity (For example, "We'll do that at 2:00"), instead of a statement of ambiguity ("We'll get to it sometime later").

11. Are there therapies available in your school system that might be beneficial for a particular inflexible-explosive student? If so, how can they be accessed?

## Chapter 12:

1. "School personnel are as prone to back-end interventions as are other adults, especially in relation to dealing with children whose frustrations cause them to disrupt the classroom process." Discuss an incident where you used a "back-end" intervention unsuccessfully in dealing with a student. What could have been done differently?

2. Read the Q and A section on pp. 268-270. Do you agree or disagree with the following statements? Discuss.

   • Kids who aren't inflexible-explosive will become inflexible-explosive if exposed to kids who are.

   • When we continue to apply strategies that don't work, we send a message to students that we can't help them.

   • Inflexible-explosive kids can learn and practice behaviors better in school than when suspended from school.

   • Students who are administered ineffective consequences over the course of years become more alienated from society.

   • Schools, not just parents, are obligated to work with and help students who are inflexible-explosive.

   • Jail is the ultimate back-end intervention.

   • Other students can help students who are inflexible-explosive.

3. "A user-friendlier school environment would be one in which all the adults who interact with a child have a clear understanding of his unique difficulties." How could you make this happen in your school? When? Where? Who could be involved?

4. Do you accept the fact that homework may need to be altered for kids who are inflexible-explosive? Why or why not? Are you aware of which of your students and families are agonizing over homework? How can you foster good communication on homework issues with parents? How can you adapt homework assignments for particular students/families who struggle with this? Discuss specifics. Discuss the following statement: "Inflexibility-explosiveness is as good a reason to adapt school work as any other disability" (p. 274).

5. Discuss the following statement: "A user friendlier school environment would also be one in which adults try to identify – in advance – specific situations that may routinely lead to inflexible-explosive episodes." Can you identify specific incidents that trigger inflexible-explosive behavior in your students?

6.  "In a user friendlier school environment, adults read the warning signals and take quick action when these signals are present" (p. 276). What are some warning signals your inflexible-explosive student gives you? What is your plan of action?

7.  Discuss the following statement: "In a user friendlier environment, adults can interpret incoherent behaviors for what they really are: incoherent behaviors" (p. 277). Are you able to not take your inflexible-explosive student's outbursts personally or as a personal affront to your authority? What do you think your student is really trying to say? Practice responding to students who are refusing to comply to one of your requests.

8.  "In a user friendlier school environment, adults can also understand how they themselves may be fueling a student's inflexibility-explosiveness." Discuss incidents where you may have done this and an alternative way the situation could have been handled.

9.  "In a user friendlier school environment, adults try to use a more accurate common language to describe various elements of the student's inflexibility-explosiveness." Make a list of unhelpful descriptive vocabulary and another list of useful vocabulary to describe a student of yours.

10. Discuss/list things you could personally do to create a classroom responsive to the needs of an inflexible-explosive student.

11. "Fair does not always mean equal." Discuss this statement in relation to your interactions with students in the classroom. What could your response be if one student asks why another student is getting special accommodations and help?

## Chapter 13:

1.  Under what circumstances do you feel it would be appropriate to have a child placed in a residential facility? What options do you have in your community?

## Chapter 14:

1.  "Children do well if they can." "Children do well if they want to." Discuss the difference between these two philosophies and the implications for each in the classroom.

## *Jackson Whole Wyoming* by Joan Clark
## Learning Team Study Discussion Questions (Asperger Syndrome)

**Chapter 1:**

Describe Tyler's mixed feelings regarding being recognized as Jackson's friend. What are his fears? Did his teacher recognize his feelings and handle them appropriately? Are there any other suggestions on how she could have handled the situation?

**Chapter 2:**

Obsessive compulsive behavior such as Jackson's rigid way of placing his crayons in the box can be characteristic of people with Asperger Syndrome (AS). What evidence of OCD do you see in your students with AS? Do you think they can help or control this?

**Chapter 3:**

Schedule changes and transitions are difficult for students with AS. Is there something Jackson's classroom teacher and speech teacher could have done differently to make the speech class time more productive? What can be done in our classrooms to make transitions easier for these kids?

**Chapter 4:**

Obsessions and an inability to follow instructions can be disruptive in the classroom and it's important that kids with AS learn to follow teacher instructions despite these issues. Notice how obsessions, intense focus, and interest in the fan indicate Jackson's intelligence in the workings of mechanical items. How can this focus and aptitude be allowed and encouraged in the classroom without being a disruption? Can you think of similar, specific situations with your students with AS?

**Chapter 5:**

Mrs. Howard seems unaware of Jackson's AS characteristics. Where in the chapter can you see the following illustrated?

    A. Insistence on following the "rules"

B. Inability to understand idioms

C. Going off into "another world" to escape stress

Do you see these same characteristics in any of your students with AS? What can we do as teachers to help them better understand the world around them?

## Chapter 6:

Jackson's area of special interest is monkeys. It is common for kids with AS to have areas of special interest. Are you familiar with your kids' areas of special interest? How can we encourage this kind of extensive knowledge and at the same time teach when others are tired of hearing about them? If peers aren't educated about AS, they often stay away from students who have this condition, fearing their "different-ness." Sometimes they even think they are retarded if they don't have the opportunity to get to know them. Kids respect intelligence in their peers. How can we provide opportunities to showcase the knowledge kids with AS possess? How can we challenge them to prevent boredom in the classroom? When career counseling older students, how can we match up areas of special interest with possible future careers?

## Chapter 7:

Adults have a strong influence on how kids who are different are viewed by their peers. Despite her frustration, how might Mrs. Smithers' eye rolling and lack of understanding of Jackson's communication difficulties have added "fuel to the fire" in his peers' non-acceptance of his unique behaviors? How could she have handled the crayon incident differently? Are you aware of how both your verbal and nonverbal interactions with kids with AS when you are frustrated can have a negative effect on the classroom environment?

Tyler makes a common assumption when he thinks that because Jackson doesn't make outward attempts to be his friend (not trying to get his attention on the bus) that he has no desire to have friends. Kids with AS often want friends, but have no idea how to go about making them. How can we help create situations in the school environment where we can teach both kids with AS and their peers to interact with one another?

## Chapter 8:

Tyler's mom and Miss Wilson join forces to intervene and talk to Tyler about what AS is to help him understand both his cousin Drew and Jackson. Do you think this is an appropriate strategy? If so, how can it be used in your school? Whose role would it be to implement it?

**Chapter 9:**

It is common for kids who were previously kind to kids with AS in elementary school to either ignore them or become openly teasing and hostile in middle school. Why do you think this happens? What can we do about it at school? Should we intervene or "let nature take its course"?

**Chapter 10:**

Miss Wilson says she can't talk about Jackson's condition because it's a private thing. Do you agree or disagree? What would be the advantages of informing peers of the condition of a particular student with AS? What would be the disadvantages? Fortunately, in the story Tyler has a cousin with AS that he is able to learn about. Most of your students won't have that opportunity. Do we educate peers about the condition, or not? If yes, how do we do this?

**Chapter 11:**

Miss Berg made Jackson important and respected in the eyes of his peers. How did she do that? How can we do this for our kids with AS?

**Chapter 12:**

Jackson thinks Marcus is his friend. It's common for kids with AS to not recognize when they are being teased or bullied. What can we do to keep our classrooms safe environments for all our kids?

**Chapter 13:**

Kids with AS can be very rule-oriented and have difficulty knowing when rules can be bent and when they cannot. What example of this is illustrated when Mr. Carson is guest speaker? Do you see this in any of your students with AS? What ideas do you have to minimize classroom distractions when these students get "stuck"?

It's common for kids with AS to comment on physical appearances, even when it's inappropriate. How can we help these kids learn appropriate social skills in this area?

Jackson has a strong sensory mode of interacting with his world. How does his teacher redirect and substitute appropriate ways to use his sense of touch in the classroom? Is this something your students could benefit from? What other items could they use to substitute putting fingers in their mouths, picking things up off the floor and smelling them, chewing objects, etc., that would be appropriate?

## Chapter 14:
Students with AS often have difficulty understanding the perceptions of others and delaying their own gratification. Jackson couldn't understand that the other boy wanted the pinwheel just as much as he did and was rude until he got what he wanted. Do you see similarities in your students with AS? Whose role is it to teach manners and how can this be done in the regular classroom?

## Chapters 15-17:
Jackson is unable to tell lies, a common characteristic of students with AS. How can this be a positive attribute, and when can it cause problems in your classroom?

## Chapter 18:
Tyler realizes that he and Jackson are not "real" friends. He doesn't invite him over outside of school or interact with him the way he does with his true friends. Do you think kids with AS are capable of knowing what a true friend is? Do they realize they may not have true friends? Is it important to have students in your classrooms behave as if they were friends, even if they aren't in the true sense of the word? If yes, how can that be encouraged?

## Chapters 19-20:
Tyler recognizes that Marcus bullies Jackson and feels bad for not having stepped up in the past to defend him. Brainstorm ways to give our kids the tools and confidence necessary to stand up to bullies like Marcus.

## Chapter 21:
Tyler's poem is full of characteristics kids with AS have in common. How has reading this book helped you understand your students with AS better?

## *Joey Pigza Swallowed the Key*
## Learning Team Discussion Questions (ADD)

**Chapter 1:**

Joey mentions he was O.K. in the morning, but that after lunch when his meds had worn down he lost control. A debate has gone on for years on whether ADD is a legitimate condition or just an excuse for behavior that a child can control. What are your personal beliefs/experiences regarding the ADD/medication issue?

The following steps were taken to deal with Joey's out-of-control behavior: (a) verbal prompt to "settle down," (b) removal from class, (c) when disruptive in hall told to settle down for five minutes and then rejoin class, (d) sent to the principal to sort crayons. Do you think this was effective? Is there anything that could have been done differently?

**Chapter 2:**

Joey talks about his family tree of ADD. Research shows that ADD can run in families, lending credence to the idea that it could have genetic or environmental causes. Do you believe genetics or environment causes ADD?

ADD does not disappear when a child grows up and leaves school; it may just manifest itself differently. What evidence could indicate that Joey's grandmother has adult ADD? Do you know adults who show these tendencies?

**Chapter 3:**

Every classroom has rules, but Mrs. Maxy's were ineffective with Joey. Why? Can you think of a better way rules could be taught to kids with ADD?

Discuss elements of classroom communication that could be problematic for students with ADD. Are there alternative ways to communicate that might be more effective?

As illustrated in this chapter, medications can be very beneficial for children with ADD, but they are not 100% effective all the time. Discuss what you know about ADD medications, including positive benefits and drawbacks.

**Chapter 4:**

Joey mentions that he could pay attention when his teacher read *The Great Gilly Hopkins*. Some people believe that if a child can pay attention to some things, such as playing a video game for long periods of time, they could not possibly have ADD and instead just choose when to attend. But this may not be accurate. Kids with ADD are often able to pay attention when an activity is constantly, immediately reinforcing for them. Can you think of some activities you have seen that keep your kids with ADD on task?

Joey's mom gave him a picture to use as a cue/prompt to calm him down. Can you think of other items that could be used with your distracted students? Describe what goes on in the mind of a child with ADD when bombarded with multiple questions or directions.

Having to accept special education services can initially be difficult and even traumatic for students who need them. Describe Joey's feelings. Could the adults have made it easier for him? How?

**Chapter 5:**

Taking medications consistently is essential for kids like Joey, but sometimes parents forget due to the "busyness" of life, or even because they may have ADD and organizational issues themselves. Is there any way the school can help?

Describe what it is like for Joey to try to read a book when he's forgotten to take his meds. How can continual, inconsistent medication result in educational deficiencies? Have you seen this in your students? What can educators do to fill in these gaps?

**Chapter 6:**

Sugar seemed to be a factor in Joey's getting more out of control, and it is understandable that his teacher did not want him to have any of the pie. Could her decision to not let him eat the pie (and not to let him have a pumpkin carving knife like the other kids) have been handled differently?

Mrs. Maxy says, "It's just that there is always a difference between what you think you are doing and what happens to you and everyone else," to indicate her frustration with Joey's lack of impulse control. Does this ever manifest itself in some of your students with ADD?

**Chapter 7:**

Although Joey's ADD and lack of impulse control result in disastrous consequences, his intentions are good. If we were able to get inside the minds of some of our students, it might be easier to understand their behavior and acknowledge and appreciate their strengths and the motivations behind some of the things they do. Are you able to find strengths and verbally recognize them? How can we make a conscious effort to praise even the most difficult of our students?

**Chapter 8:**

The decision has been made to send Joey to a special school and for him to receive mandatory counseling. Do you think this is a good decision? Why or why not? Do you think his mother's feelings are justified? Why or why not?

**Chapter 9:**

Maria's father blames Joey's mother for Joey's behavior. When kids misbehave, teachers at times have a tendency to do the same. Is this productive? What can we do to redirect and what should we focus on instead? What kind of mother is Joey's mom? Do you believe the parents of your more challenged kids love and want the best for them? How can we better function as a team with the parents of our behaviorally challenged kids?

**Chapter 10:**

What are your first impressions of the special school Joey is sent to? More and more schools are adopting a full inclusion model for children with all types of disabilities. What are the advantages of full inclusion? What are the challenges?

"Special Ed" doesn't do a good job of listening to Joey to discover what his fears are and what his emotional state is. Sometimes we have to deal with the feelings and emotions of our students before we can begin to teach them. What could Ed do differently? What can we do to better tune into our kids who are struggling?

**Chapter 11:**

Ed from Joey's special school indicates to Joey that his home life is a contributing factor to his behavioral condition. What environmental challenges does Joey have in addition to his medical condition? Do any of your students have these combined challenges? How can we compensate with stability at school?

Mrs. Maxy stops by to bring Joey's school work from his home school so he can keep up and not be behind when he returns from his temporary placement. Do you have students who are removed from your classroom for extended periods of time? What can you do to make the move to and from special placements as seamless as possible?

The doctor treats Joey as if he has a medical and behavioral condition that requires multiple diagnostic tests in order to prescribe appropriate medication. Do you view ADD as a condition that affects the brain? Are you familiar with any current research in this area?

## Chapter 12:

Would you describe Joey's grandmother as abusive when she tried to control Joey's behavior by lying about his mother being abusive? Do you think this resulted in Joey's compulsive hair-pulling behavior? Do you see evidence of this type of self-abusing behavior in any of your students? What is a teacher's responsibility if she observes it?

Joey acknowledges his anger towards his mother for abandoning him. Do any of your students demonstrate excessive anger in the classroom? What could be the causes? Often angry children have difficulty processing and understanding their anger. Is it any wonder it can spill out into the school environment? How can you deal with anger in your students?

## Chapter 13:

Joey's life is further complicated by his not having access to his father. How do you think this plays a role in his behavior?

## Chapter 14:

The doctor takes a wholistic approach to Joey's condition, mentioning the need to attend to proper medication, family conditions, and behavior therapies. Are all three areas addressed for your students with ADD? What part do schools play in the treatment plan of children with ADD?

The doctor tells Joey it's important he gives feedback on how he's feeling on his new medication so they can continue to monitor his treatment. Is there a way schools can give feedback that would be helpful to parents and doctors in the treatment plan?

Joey's mom says, "I just like people who like you." Do the parents of your students with ADD know you like them and see their strengths and unique personalities? Is this important? How can you accomplish this?

**Chapter 15:**

Near the end of the book, one of the moms in the special ed. class told Joey, "... the medication has slowed you down, but you have been a good kid all along. You are naturally good. I hope you know that about yourself. You have a good heart." Do your students know that about themselves? How can we make sure ALL of our kids do?

# *The Curious Incident of the Dog in the Night-Time*[3] by Mark Haddon
## Learning Team Study Discussion Questions
## (Asperger Syndrome-Teenagers)

1. Christopher, the main character in this book, has Asperger Syndrome (AS), a mild form of autism. Through this description of himself, the way he relates information regarding the death of his neighbor's dog, and his communication with the police officer in the first few pages of this book, what does the reader learn are some characteristics of AS?

2. What kinds of difficulties did Christopher have communicating with the police? How could the police officer's communication with Christopher (pp. 6-8) have been more effective? Do you experience communication difficulties with your students with AS? Can you think of techniques that could be used to foster good communication?

3. Kids with AS sometimes have "areas of special interest," topics they know a lot about, obsess on, and like to talk about. What do you think are some of Christopher's? Do you know the areas of special interest of your students? Are there ways we as teachers can guide students as they prepare to make the transition from high school to the adult world, whether it be college or the world of work, utilizing their areas of special interest? How can educators keep a student with extensive knowledge in a subject area from becoming bored in class?

4. On p. 14, Christopher mentions that there are two things about people that are confusing to him. What are they? Can you find evidence of these same difficulties in your kids with AS? Do you have any ideas how to help them in the classroom comprehend body language and metaphors?

5. Some people with AS have heightened senses so things like noise, textures, and touch bother them. How is Christopher affected? Are you aware if any of your students with AS have similar characteristics?

---

[3] *Be aware some profanities are used in this book.*

6.  What does Christopher say about lying? (p. 19) Why could reading novels be difficult for your students with AS?

7.  Describe Christopher's aversion to people making eye contact (pp. 22-23). Have you noticed poor eye contact in your students with AS? Do you think this is something they need to be taught to do? Why? How?

8.  On p. 24, Christopher talks about liking things to be orderly. Do you see evidence of this need in your students with AS?

9.  How does Christopher feel about rules? (p. 29) Have you had disruptions in your classes when kids with AS don't understand rules or are overly rigid when it comes to others following rules? How do you handle this?

10. Christopher fixates on small visual details that most of us wouldn't even notice. Read his description of Mr. Jeavons (p. 5), the policewoman (p. 6), and the inspector (p. 17). Do you think his attention to these details gets in the way of him understanding people and their interactions with him? Do you think attention to details like this could get in the way of AS students' learning in the classroom setting? Are there ways to get their focus off small details so they are better able to attend to the learning task at hand?

11. Christopher says he does not like strangers (p. 35), and it takes him a long time to get to know people. What implications could this have for your students with AS on the days you have a substitute teacher? Is there anything that could be done to minimize possible distress?

12. People with AS can have extreme difficulty making small talk. Describe Christopher's view of "chatting" on p. 40. Learning to have conversations is an important social skill necessary in an interactive society. How can we help kids like Christopher become more comfortable with this?

13. Understanding metaphors can also be difficult for people with AS. What are the expressions Christopher says Mrs. Shears used that were confusing for him? (p. 43) As teachers working with kids with AS, it might be beneficial to explain terms like this and remember to not take for granted that they will be able to understand our communication.

14. Christopher has an interesting (and healthy) perspective of "special needs" (pp. 43-44). What is it? How can we foster greater acceptance of differences in our classrooms and promote zero tolerance for bullying?

15. Sometimes we wrestle with the idea that special needs kids get privileges other students might not receive. Do you think Christopher's father was appropriate to insist the school make an exception and let him take his A-level test in math? (pp. 44-45)

16. On pp. 45-48, Christopher describes his "behavioral problems" and the effect they have had on his parents and their marriage. He doesn't seem to express this with any emotion or understanding of how difficult his condition could be on his family. Do you think kids with AS are truly able to perceive how their actions affect others? Do they experience remorse? Do we as educators have empathy for the parents of our special needs students? Or do we tend to blame them for our students' problems? In what ways can we work more effectively as partners with our students?

17. Christopher talks about how he would like to be an astronaut so he could live without people around him (pp. 50-51). Do you see tendencies in your students with AS to want to be alone? Why do you think this is? Should we provide alone time for them during the school day? How much?

18. Christopher demonstrates compulsions and superstitions regarding his Good Days and Black Days based on the colors of cars he sees on his way to school. What was his behavior like on his Black Days? (p. 53) World views such as this may make no sense to other people; nonetheless, kids spend their bad days at school and teachers have to deal with them. What does a bad day look like for your AS students? How can we help them get through days like this?

19. Christopher says he "can't do chatting" (p. 55). Is this a necessary social skill? How can we teach kids like Christopher to hold conversations with others?

20. On p. 67 Christopher mentions not liking being laughed at by Rhodri. Why do you think that is? Have you noticed this in your students with AS?

21. What brings on Christopher's meltdown? (pp. 82-83) Was the meltdown productive? What other approaches could Christopher's father have used? Are you familiar with meltdowns your students may have? Do you know what triggers them? Are they productive? What approaches might be effective in preventing meltdowns in your students?

22. How do Christopher and his father show affection for one another? (p. 87) Do you think people with AS experience love the way people without AS do?

23. In one of her letters to Christopher, his mother states that she has been a bad mother (p. 106). Have you ever imagined the difficulties a parent of a child with AS might have? What could those be? How can we as educators show empathy to the parents of our students with AS?

24. One of Christopher's teachers told his parents that he would always find understanding other people's minds (or perspectives) difficult. What examples of this can you find in this book? Do you notice this lack of understanding the perceptions of others in your day-to-day dealings with your students with AS? How does this deficit affect your classrooms? Are there ways to minimize any possible negative outcomes due to this?

25. Christopher mentions that his head hurts because there is too much noise and too much information as he tries to find his way to the train station (p. 139). It is common for kids with AS to be especially sensitive to noise and experience "information overload." Have you noticed this in your students? How can a classroom teacher handle this?

26. Christopher mentions that he "sees everything" (p. 140). How is this an advantage? A disadvantage?

27. How does Christopher respond when he is scared because he's in an unfamiliar situation such as when he's in the train station in Swindon? (p. 145) Have you ever noticed any of your students with AS in a situation that was frightening to them? How did they respond? How did it affect the educational environment? Are you aware of calming strategies that are effective for your students?

28. Sometimes people with AS are unable to understand jokes and humorous situations. Christopher says that he doesn't like it when people laugh. Why do you think that would be? Have you noticed times when your students have had difficulty recognizing humorous situations?

29. Christopher describes not liking when his family goes to France on holiday because "when people are on holiday they don't have a timetable" (p. 156). It's common for people with AS to experience anxiety when schedules change. Have you noticed this in your students? What can we do in the school environment to prevent problems?

30. People with AS often find being in places with lots of people a negative experience. Christopher describes what it is like for him to have so many people with him on the train (p. 158). What times/places throughout the school day might be stressful for students with AS due to the noise and commotion? Are there things that could be done to minimize this exposure?

31. It seems surprising that Christopher has incredible knowledge in academic subjects such as mathematics, but gaps in life skills knowledge, as evidenced in his not knowing how to ask for a restroom on the train and subsequently wetting himself. Even very intelligent kids with AS need to be taught life skills that most of us take for granted and learn very naturally. How can schools help teach life skills to students so they can function independently in society as they grow up?

32. Christopher does math puzzles in his head to help him deal with the stress of traveling alone (p. 166). Do your kids with AS have effective calming strategies they can use when they start to experience stress? If not, brainstorm some things you might teach them to try.

33. Printed words appear jumbled and incomprehensible to Christopher (pp. 169-170). He comments that his "brain wasn't working properly" as a result of stressors. When your students with AS are frightened and stressed, is your lesson the most important thing at that moment? What can be done to bring them back to maximum learning potential? Can teachers force a student in this state to learn?

34. Christopher demonstrates safety issues in the subway station (pp. 182-183). Do your students with AS have similar gaps in terms of how to stay safe? How is this dealt with in your school?

35. When Christopher's mother discovered how he had been told she was dead and the manner in which the truth was revealed (p. 193), she responded with emotions and wailing that Christopher didn't understand. How can we teach students with AS to identify and comprehend the emotions of others?

36. How does Mr. Shears show a total lack of understanding of Christopher's condition? (p. 207) Are there people in your school community who have similar views of students with AS? What can be done to help them understand the unique challenges and strengths of these kids?

37. At the end of the book, Christopher describes his plans for the future. What do you think your students with AS are capable of doing when they grow up? What can you do to help them get there?

# CONCLUSION

## Meet Cassie

Cassie is a talented actress, poet, photographer, artist, and public speaker, who loves to play basketball and attend school dances. She's a good student, a "joiner," an optimist, and one of the most friendly, upbeat people I've ever known. Cassie also struggles with tics from Tourette Syndrome, which, in addition to causing her body to seemingly be in perpetual motion, makes holding a pen and writing nearly impossible at times. Because of her obsessive compulsive disorder, Cassie's hands tap on her desk in endless patterns understood only by her, and she has constant, daily battles to avoid continually staring at whichever boy she is infatuated with at the time. In what seems to be an even more unfair twist of fate, Cassie has also recently been diagnosed with Asperger Syndrome, which explains her need to have even the simplest social skills deliberately taught. Cassie was one of those students who felt increasingly alienated when she entered the "middle school social jungle."

The programs outlined in this book have been a life line for Cassie and others like her in our school. She eats lunch at a table full of kids every day, engaging in teenage conversations, just like everyone else. She is as busy as any other high school student, whether she's auditioning for the spring play after school, playing on her coed intramural basketball team in the evening, or spending an entire day at a speech competition or an overnight at a thespian convention. She feels comfortable dancing with kids at a high school dance and hanging out in the halls in between classes.

None of this happened by accident. A Circle of Friends was developed, monitored, and adjusted when necessary. A counselor from outside of school as well as support staff in the school have painstakingly taught Cassie the myriad social skills that continually present challenges for her. Caring peers reach out to her on a daily basis. The adults in her school community have taken the time to read about her condition and brainstorm the best ways to help her reach her full potential.

The benefits a supportive school community yields are well worth the effort. It only takes one person to get the ball rolling, and the rewards are immeasurable.

Good luck implementing the concepts outlined in this book. And … thanks in advance from the Cassies in your school.

## A Problem
## By Cassie Gabel – age 14

People don't understand.
They don't know
How someone feels
About having a problem
Called Aspergers.
It's hard,
Socially
And emotionally.
A problem
That screams inside,
"Why can't I be normal?"
"Why?"
I scream,
Holding on,
Onto the ride;
I don't know what's coming,
Or where I'm going.
Will I be slammed
Into a brick wall?
Making a fool of myself,
And of my family,
Making things worse
Than they already are.
I hope not,
I really do.
I have hope
That people will understand
Everything,
And anything,
About me,
And my problem.

## Different
## By Cassie Gabel

People say they can make a basket in a basketball game easily,

And it's easy to be consistent.

I say it's easier to make a shot in practice,

And every shot is different for me.

I guess I'm just that.

Different.

A different thinker,

A different game player,

A different person.

At least I never thought I was weird,

But that's what people call me.

Weird.

It sounds different to me when other people say it.

I feel it's only another way to encourage myself,

To be better than I am,

To be better than myself.

Others see it as a way to give them something,

Something to talk about,

Something to laugh about,

Something to say.

I'm different.

I don't have a problem being that way.

At least I know what loving someone and being kind is.

If I were the same as them,

There wouldn't even be a me.

And I wouldn't be special.

Now I won't worry about who I'm not.

I'll be who I am.

Even if I do only make baskets in practice.

# REFERENCES

Frederickson, N., & Turner, J. (2001). Utilising the classroom peer group to address children's social needs. An evaluation of the 'Circles of Friends' intervention approach. *Exceptional Child, 14,* 234-245.

Attwood, T. (1998). *Asperger Syndrome: A guide for parents and professionals.* New York: Jessica Kingsley Publishers.

The Gray Center for Social Learning and Understanding, http://www.thegraycenter.org/socialstories.cfm

Roberts, S. M., & Pruitt, E. Z. (2003). *Schools as professional learning communities: Collaborative activities and strategies for professional development.* Thousand Oaks, CA: Corwin Press.

# Bibliography

## *Book Club Novels for Students*

Bennett, V. (2003). *Monkey*. New York: Walker Books.

Covington, D. (1993). *Lizard*. New York: Laurel Leaf Books.

Draper, S. (2002). *Double Dutch*. New York: Anthenaeum Books for Young Readers.

Gilson, J. (2003). *Hello, My Name Is Scrambled Eggs*. New York: Aladdin Paperbacks.

Hesser, S. (1999). *Kissing Doorknobs*. New York: Bantam Doubleday Dell Books for Young Readers.

Katz, J . (2001). *Geeks*. Portland, OR: Broadway Books.

Keith, L. (1997). *A Different Life*. New York: Livewire.

Konigsburg, E. L. (1996). *The View from Saturday*. New York: Atheneum Books for Young Readers.

Levine, G. (2001). *The Wish*. New York: Harper Trophy.

Peck, R. (1987). *Princess Ashley*. New York: Delacorte Press.

Philbrick, R. (1993). *Freak the Mighty*. New York: Scholastic.

Sachar, L. (1987). *There's a Boy in the Girl's Bathroom*. New York: Knopf-Random House.

Spinelli, J. (2002). *Loser*. New York: Joanna Cotler Books.

Spinelli, J. (2004). *Stargirl*. New York: Dell Laurel-Leaf.

Trueman, T. (2003). *Stuck in Neutral*. New York: Harper Tempest.

White, R. (2002). *Memories of Summer*. New York: Dell Laurel-Leaf.

Willis, K. (2001). *When Zachary Beaver Came to Town*. New York: Dell Yearling.

Willner-Pardo, G. (1999). *Figuring out Francis*. Dennison, CO: Clarion Books.

## *Circle Meeting Activities*

http://educationworld.com

http://kimscorner4teachertalk.com

http://midhudson.org/program/ideas/Icebreaker_Activities_Kids.rtf

http://sdces.sdstate.edu/cld/files/ice%20breaker%20ideas.pdf

http://www.cplrmh.com/icebreakers.html

## *Additional Book Club Novel Study Guides*

Ellen Gabor's Ellen's Teaching Made Easier:  http://www.e-tme.com

Mary Schlieder's Schools with Open Arms: http://schoolswithopenarms.com


## *Learning Team Books*

Buron, K. (2006). *A 5 Is Against the Law! Social Boundaries: Straight Up! An Honest Guide for Teens and Adults*. Shawnee Mission, KS: Autism Asperger Publishing.

Clark J. (2002). *Jackson Whole Wyoming*. Shawnee Mission, KS: Autism Asperger Publishing.

Gantos, J. (1998). *Joey Pigza Swallowed the Key*. New York: Farrar, Straus, & Giroux.

Greene, R. (2001). *The Explosive Child*. New York: Harper Collins Publishers.

Haddon, M. (2003). *The Curious Incident of the Dog in the Night-Time*. New York: Vintage Books.


## *Additional Learning Team Book Study Guides*

Mary Schlieder's Schools with Open Arms: http://schoolswithopenarms.com

## *General References*

Frederickson, N., & Turner, J. (2001). Utilising the classroom peer group to address children's social needs. An evaluation of the 'Circles of Friends' intervention approach. *Exceptional Child, 14*, 234-245.

Greenway, C. (n.d.). Autism and Asperger Syndrome: Strategies to promote prosocial behavior. *Educational Psychology in Practice, 16*(4), 469-486.

Levison, L., & St. Onge, I. (1999). *Disability Awareness in the Classroom: A Resource Tool for Teachers and Students*. Springfield, IL: Charles C. Thomas Publisher.

Newton, C., Taylor, G., & Wilson, D. (1996). Circle of Friends: An inclusive approach to meeting emotional and behavioral difficulties. *Educational Psychology in Practice, 11*, 41-48.

Perski, R. (1998). Circles of Friends. Nashville, TN: Abingdon Press.

ter, M.A., Johnstun, M., & Munk, J.A. (2005) From Spaceman to ADDed Touch: Using Juvenile Literature to teach about Attention Deficit Hyperactivity Disorder. *TEACHING Exceptional Children Plus*, 1(4) Article 4. Retrieved May 31, 2007, from http://escholarship.bc.edu/education/tecplus/

Schloff, L., & Yudkin, M. (1991). *Smart Speaking*. New York: Penguin Books.

Taylor, G. (1997). Community building in schools: Developing a Circle of Friends. *Educational & Child Psychology*, *14*, 45-50.

### Learning Team Books

Clark J. (2005). *Jackson Whole Wyoming*. Shawnee Mission, KS: Autism Asperger Publishing.

Gantos, J. (1998). *Joey Pigza Swallowed the Key*. New York: Farrar, Straus, & Giroux.

Greene, R. (2001). *The Explosive Child*. New York: Harper Collins Publishers.

Haddon, M. (2003). *The Curious Incident of the Dog in the Night-Time*. New York: Vintage Books.

# APC

Autism Asperger Publishing Co.
P.O. Box 23173
Shawnee Mission, Kansas 66283-0173
www.asperger.net